TOP BILLIN'

BILL BELLAMY

WITH NICOLE E. SMITH

TOP BILLIN'

STORIES OF LAUGHTER, LESSONS, AND TRIUMPH

AMISTAD

An Imprint of HarperCollins*Publishers*

HarperCollins books may be purchased for educational, business, or sales promotional use. For information, please email the Special Markets Department at
SPsales@harpercollins.com.

FIRST EDITION

Library of Congress Cataloging-in-Publication Data

Names: Bellamy, Bill, 1965- author. | Smith, Nicole E., author.
Title: Top billin' : stories of laughter, lessons, and triumph / Bill Bellamy ; with
    Nicole E. Smith.
Description: First edition. | New York : HarperCollins, 2023.
Identifiers: LCCN 2022043080 (print) | LCCN 2022043081 (ebook) | ISBN
    9780063237629 (hardcover) | ISBN 9780063237636 (trade paperback) | ISBN
    9780063237643 (ebook)
Subjects: LCSH: Bellamy, Bill, 1965- | Comedians—United States—Biography. |
    African American actors—Biography. | Video jockeys—Biography. |
    Nineteen nineties. | LCGFT: Autobiographies.
Classification: LCC PN2287.B415 A3 2023 (print) | LCC PN2287.B415 (ebook) |
    DDC 792.702/8092 [B]--dc23/eng/20230210
LC record available at https://lccn.loc.gov/2022043080
LC ebook record available at https://lccn.loc.gov/2022043081

---

23 24 25 26 27 LBC 5 4 3 2 1

I dedicate these words of love and self-discovery to my dearly departed parents, Edna and William Bellamy Sr. Thank you for making me the man I was born to be.

I also dedicate these pages to my wife, Kristen Barker Bellamy, and kids, Bailey Ivory-Rose and Baron Bellamy. With your love, I became the man I never knew I could be.

Loving you always and forever!

CONTENTS

FOREWORD

I first became aware of Bill Bellamy when we were both college students at Rutgers University in our home state of New Jersey. I do not even think I knew he was an aspiring comedian at the time. I recall that Bill was tall, lean, and handsome. A very serious man with his fashion tastes, he often wore penny loafer shoes with argyle socks, as we did back then, and he could dance as well as anyone at RU. I saw Bill around campus often. He always had an infectious smile, and was always full of life. But I did not know that he was a comedian until one year during our mutual time in college he was the entertainment at a Black Greek-lettered step show.

Back then I was still terrified of ever considering being on any stage, so I was in awe that one of my peers, Bill, so effortlessly ran through joke after joke to much laughter and applause. Little did I know, at that time, that Bill Bellamy was well on his way to becoming one of several Black comedians deeply inspired by pop culture, hip-hop, and social issues, coupled with an acute awareness that forebears Richard Pryor and Eddie Murphy had already kicked in the door.

As fate would have it I, an ambitious young writer, would be picked to be a cast member on the very first season of MTV's *The Real World* in New York City. The show became a huge hit and Bill Bellamy would arrive at the network shortly thereafter, to host *MTV Jams* and various other shows for what was then the single most important network for young people on the planet. I knew Bill was blazing his trail with comedy, because I had been following him on things like Russell Simmons's *Def Comedy Jam* on HBO. But with MTV Bill became a certifiable star, a celebrity, a pop culture icon. And in the 1990s, he likewise instantly was part of the explosion of Black culture, which included him, Queen Latifah, Chris Rock, Martin Lawrence, Will Smith, the Wayans family, Lauryn Hill, and Dave Chappelle.

I was proud to say I knew Bill Bellamy from way back, proud of his successes, as he made his way through television, through films, while staying true to his great passion for live stand-up comedy. Bill does not know that I've watched pretty much whatever he has done from the jump. When he appeared somewhere I felt like he was representing me and every Black boy from our backgrounds. Because there is something special, something magical, about seeing another Black male from our home state of New Jersey make a name for himself. Bill Bellamy is a hero to more people than he will ever know.

And there is also something to be said for the fact that Bill has methodically stayed true to himself, to his value system, as a man, as a husband, as a father, taking the time, despite the countless temptations of Hollywood, to make sure he represented for his family. Indeed that, to me, is the most powerful part of his story, on top of his own humble beginnings in

Newark, New Jersey; the traumas he had to overcome to get to and through an elite private high school in Jersey—Seton Hall Prep; what he thought his life was going to be with his economics major at Rutgers, yet finding his true calling because of his unique gift to bring joy to the masses. Bill, yes, is mad funny, but he is also humble, wise, and someone who takes very seriously his responsibility not just to make folks laugh, but to be a role model, a bridge, on how to make it and thrive in a business that is so wildly unpredictable, and so wildly unfair for so many.

To be sure, Bill Bellamy is not just someone who has survived much, but he is a winner because he has done it on his own terms. His life journey is a grand and honest testimony to not only the things we must and can overcome, but also to the greatest possibilities of the human spirit if we simply believe in ourselves.

Kevin Powell
Poet, Journalist, Civil and Human Rights Activist
Brooklyn, New York

PROLOGUE

I remember having a dream when I was in the sixth grade that I was driving a school bus and the passengers were the legendary singing group *The Jackson 5*. They all knew me, and I felt like I really knew them too. We were all on a field trip laughing and joking like brothers. How is it possible that later in my life, not only would I meet them all, but I would be hand-picked to interview the King of Pop himself in front of the entire world?

Remember, there are no coincidences in life. None!

Buckle up! You're about to enter into a journey through my life. Through a time that saw the rise and fall of the music scene as we knew it in the 1990s. My life, my story, and my legacy are all undeniably interwoven with the music that shaped today's culture. I dream in verse. To help you understand me and what I was going through at various phases in my life, I open up each chapter with a different song title. Nothing evokes memories, or cements them in the archives, like great music. True to nature, I approached this memoir as somewhat of a soundtrack to my life. Some parts rough and tumultuous, others smooth sailing.

Sit back, reminisce with me, and enjoy reliving some of the key moments that make this Newark, New Jersey, native the legendary Bill Bellamy!

See you on the flip side.

THE MAKING OF A BILL

"LOVE AND HAPPINESS"

Song by Al Green

Before there was the cool, funny, charismatic well-dressed Bill Bellamy, there was the poor, frustrated, soda-slinging William Bellamy that had to claw his way out of the ghetto. This is the story of how I found myself and found my way to fame without losing William or my soul.

* * *

My mother had me when she was sixteen. She never finished high school, but to this day Edna Hall will always be one of the smartest, most insightful people I have ever known. My dad was nineteen, or so he said. I'm not going to lie; the math's a bit fuzzy around that story. And, if you judge by today's standards, he was fishing in the danger zone. Just like many people's parents, they were two young kids who got caught up messing around. They were out there doing grown folks' business with grown folks' results. That's how my melon head popped into the world on April 7, 1965. William Bellamy Jr.

Edna Hall and William Bellamy Sr. met in high school in a small town called Cottondale, Florida. Edna was a cute little sassy and voluptuous brown-skinned beauty that had a mouth that far exceeded her years. She was slicktalking and fast walking. She was funny as hell and that's where I think I got a lot of my character. Even though she was a tough cookie on the outside, Mom was soft, warm, and fiercely protective. My dad, William, took you by surprise. He was a manly man and an extremely hard-working dude. Inside he was warm, gentle, tender, and loving. He was very much a nurturer, which was not typical for men of his time. In those days many women often married the first guy they dated. Women were taught to wait patiently to be pursued and be happy when they snagged a good man. The next hurdle was to pray he'd make an honest woman out of them. Southern ways for Southern days.

In the early sixties my dad left the South, driving up to New York with his cousin, because everybody said there were a whole lot of job opportunities up there. Yep, he was part of the Southern exodus. People on the move for the promise of a life of prosperity and happiness; a life of nothing but milk and honey. Finding that he liked it up North, Dad boldly asked my mom and her girlfriend to join him and a friend of his in New Jersey. They did it like that back then. My grandmother Mineola

Hall, or Minnie as folks called her, didn't skip a beat. In her eyes, my dad was a catch and a good choice for my mom. Back then you were seen as a rock star if you made it to the North. These folks were perceived as explorers and conquerors of new worlds. Real Christopher Columbus shit. In her true country way, Minnie prodded my mom, saying, "Girl, you better go up there. That man want you up there! You betta not drag your feet girl." You know how them old country–ass folks talked. Obviously, my dad did want my mother because I was born within a year of her making it to New Jersey. In the words of the 1990s group Tag Team, "Whoomp there it is!"

There they were: these two young kids, with a kid, who didn't know their heads from their asses. My mom was not even a senior in high school; she was a baby herself who now had a baby. I can only imagine how deep and scary as hell that must have been for her. Nobody knew what they were doing. Everybody was young, trying to figure it out on the fly. My mom never went back down South to live. She stayed up North with my dad and got a job to now help support the family. From what I understand, here came Grandma Mineola again, and she told my dad, "It's time to make that girl a 'good woman' and get married, William. I don't want that baby out there with no name." When your girl's mamma said it's time, you didn't argue; whether you were ready or not. It was about honor and respect back in those days. If you found yourself caught up, you were expected to do right by the girl and stand up like a man. As they say, you do the crime; you do the time. And so, Edna Hall became a "good woman" by becoming Edna Bellamy on October 2, 1966, at the Justice of the Peace. They did away with all the formalities and fancy wedding stuff. As you guessed, time was of the essence because of my mom's condition, and money was scarce for a young couple. Signed, sealed, and delivered, the deed was done.

Newark, New Jersey: aka Brick City. They called it Brick City because there were so many red and brown brick apartment buildings that they swallowed up all other types of structures or patches of green space. A homogenous and cramped inner-city playground of strong towering structures and even stronger people. Looking back, it seemed like it was always cloudy and overcast in my city, which was partly due to the endless smokestacks that littered the landscape. Our haze-covered city offered its inhabitants subpar living-wage jobs that ensured that the poor stayed poor and in their zip code. These were resilient blue-collar Brown and Black people that looked like me. People that literally lived and breathed all the limitations that Newark had to offer. My mother, even without a high school education, latched on to a factory job, working at a pharmaceutical company called Novartis Sandoz. She eventually worked her way up to a bigger position where she was head of production in the factory. She became the boss. She was the person that was managing all the lines with all types of drugs running down the conveyor belts.

We lived in a two-bedroom apartment with a small kitchen and one bathroom with an old-school cast iron tub in it. When we would get out of the tub you'd always have to make sure you didn't put your hand on the exposed radiator, which would hiss and pop. Trust me, you only had to make that mistake once to learn how to maneuver in that small space.

On the streets that made up our tightly packed neighborhood, everybody parked bumper-to-bumper. Everything seemed so cramped, so confined, and always under stress. We didn't have garages attached to homes in my hood. Street after street, old-ass cars were all jammed in anywhere four wheels and an engine could fit. I don't care how shiny your car was, you were guaranteed a new little nick or scratch on it daily. The pothole-filled streets took their toll on cars just as much as the oppressive life took its toll on the people.

Coming up you knew the names of everyone who lived within the span of a few blocks. The aroma of delicious food wafting from apartment windows, representing the different cultures that made up the hood. A smell so thick you could almost taste the different dishes being cooked up and down the block because the seasonings were so heavy-handed and rich, exuding ethnic pride. The physical and cultural closeness caused us to maneuver as one big extended family. Good and bad news traveled from house to house like lightning. I mean whether it was whispered or not, your household business made it around the block before you could even make it outside. Essentially, our first taste of high-speed internet was the chatter pipeline from the stoops. Everybody became your babysitter. There were no daycares in my neck of the woods, so my parents had to rely on Miss Willie and Mrs. Sanders down the block to watch my little ass. I had five years as an only child and then my little sister, Karen, was born and finances in my house got even tighter. She and I spent most of our childhood together before my brother, Julius, came around.

Growing up in Brick City, I innately knew at a very early age that I had to be self-sufficient. Both my parents worked multiple jobs to put food on the table. They were like a revolving door of hellos and goodbyes with a few hugs and tension-releasing laughs in between. By the time I was ten or eleven, I was a latchkey kid. Having grown peoples' responsibility at an early age seemed normal to me because all my friends were doing the same thing—it's just how we rolled. I had my own shiny key that I was taught to guard with my life. I knew how to wake myself up in the morning, get dressed, and catch the bus to go to school. I would come home by myself, let myself in, and then go to the babysitter's if my parents were going to be extra late. When I was fifteen, Karen was ten, and I was taking care of her full throttle. I was picking her up from school, and making sure we both caught the right city bus together to get home. Remember, this was way before cell phones so we were riding solo for real. Like clockwork, my mom would call us on her break to make sure we got in okay. The dinner would always be there waiting, covered over on the stove for us to reheat it. Life ran like a well-oiled machine with everybody playing their role, mostly due to my mom's rigid pre-planning. Karen and I knew we had to do our homework and make sure we were right and ready for the next day to get up and do it all over again.

It was crazy to think about how much these two little people, my sister and I, managed all on our own without even thinking it was anything extraordinary. We were just living and doing what we were told to do, no questions asked, no deviations from the rules, and definitely no damn back talk about how it was supposed to run. My mom, or dad, would get home by about six or seven in the evening. Then Mom would have to sometimes leave again because she worked the night shift. With my mom working occasional nights and my dad working days they were like two ships passing in the night. Like hard-working, weather-beaten cargo ships weighed down with freight, just trying to piece together a decent life for their three kids. Undeniably, it was hectic and family time was limited, but we all still felt the love.

As a jack-of-all-trades type of laborer, my dad wasn't as con-sistent as my mom was in his job, which caused its own stress. There was never that security of a solid two-income household. Trying his best to help put food on the table, he drove trucks for a minute, was a supervisor at a warehouse, and he also did security at Wells Fargo at one point. He was a back-breaking-manual-labor sort of guy picking up any little job he could. Essentially, this dynamic made my mom the breadwinner by default in our household, which was far from the norm during those times. Earning more money than my dad, with no edu-cation, she also saved religiously by stashing money away in her 401k plan. Mom's ability to be laser-focused was her super-power, and she was a superhero to me. Somehow seeing way beyond our current circumstances, she moved in the faith and promise of what could be. Correction—what actually should have been given how hard they both worked.

My pops always had like two or three jobs going on at the same time. He taught me how to maneuver and juggle my skills to make money doing whatever I could. When I was in high school, I would have to get up at four o'clock in the morning to help him clean the bank where he had his side gig. We'd scrub all the toilets, vacuum and wax all the floors to get the place ready for opening time. Mind you, after that, I still had to go to school and put in a full day of learning. Sometimes, we switched it up and cleaned houses as well. My mom and I would do a little hustle on the weekends and take on ex-tra housekeeping jobs. I also learned to transition my expert cleaning skills into detailing cars. Hard work, and even more work, was one of the key lessons of my youth. That's what I saw and learned to do.

* * *

Music was always playing in my house. Always. It was a form of entertainment, ministry, and therapy mixed together, and a constant force in my life. A great beat has the ability to grab you, causing you to sway back and forth even before you've heard one song lyric, or hook in the actual song. That's its power. Regardless of who you are, or your circumstances, good music can creep inside your soul and leave a lasting mark on your heart. The right song can invigorate my tired body, and minister to my troubled soul with the right words. All within the same verse, great music can take you on a roller-coaster of emotions, and leave you spent! My mom constantly had the radio on and would pass the time humming and singing all the tunes that played. She loved playing records on her record player as well. I will never forget that unmistakable smell of new vinyl when you'd pull an album from its sleeve. There was something special about seeing those perfectly square cardboard photos of each artist, all lined up against the wall decorating the living room baseboard, knowing that you could slide one of those puppies out of its jacket and be transformed.

The richness of the sound that came from those records was incomparable. It allowed music to be heard as it was meant to be heard, in all its rich glory. Music's steady melody was almost like a religion in my house, and we were all deeply devoted. Early on Saturday mornings I remember having to open up all the windows to let the place air out because Mom made fish the night before. Leaving the open frying pan, with the used fish grease, on the stove overnight would cause the seasoned stench to seep into every corner and have the entire place stinking! The smell got into everything. If you happened to enter our apartment even for a minute, you'd leave smelling like greasy-ass seasoned Whiting. Then Mom would loudly proclaim, "Baby, it's time to get the Pine-Sol. We got to do a deep clean!" Like clockwork, my momma would follow that up by saying, "Ooh, go put on that Al Green album." I knew exactly what song she wanted to hear when she made that request. Al's 1972 hit song "Love and Happiness" was her favorite jam. It was a song that brought her to her happy place. That same song played on repeat day after day in my childhood apartment. On the album cover Al was dressed in all white, sitting in a majestic, peacock-like white wicker chair, his legs confidently crossed, smirking like he knew he was about to own your soul like a god!

In our little dismal corner of the world, we had clearly segregated neighborhoods. All the Black folks lived over here. All Italians lived over there, and the Spanish people lived even farther over there. Culturally, for the most part, Newark presented a very segregated existence for the most part. You knew you were Black and you better not forget it! The only hint of blending that I could see happening was with the Spanish folk on our block who acted just like us Black folk. In my eyes, the assimilation was so seamless, they weren't even Spanish anymore, they were considered Black. They lived like us, talked and sounded just like us, and acted Black. They absorbed our culture as well, yet they still spoke Spanish and loved their own culture. We in turn got a glimpse into Spanish culture and shared the same social exchange. Regardless of the color of our skin, the one thing our communities had in common was that we were all dirt poor.

Newark was geographically small, but carried a big influence on the Black cultural vernacular. Even through obvious despair in my town, there was also a buzz and energy generated by the people. You could look across the street and see Miss Johnson sitting on her stoop. You'd look up at the top window and see Miss Lilly always perched there rocking her pink sponge rollers keeping a watch over the kids on the block. She was our very own neighborhood watch and TMZ combined. Kids were constantly in the streets happily playing ball, jumping rope, doing hopscotch, and riding bikes. The sound of laughter was all around, causing our block to vibrate with pure joy. This was a sound that had nothing to do with economics or perfect living conditions, or else it would have surely passed my community by. In the summertime, good old Mr. Thompson, a fireman who lived on the block, would get his oversized wrench and crank open the fire hydrant so the neighborhood kids could run around and splash carefree in the spraying water. Even if only for a few minutes, it made us feel like we were transported to the beach. We'd spray the cold water on each other until someone from inside the building would yell out that the sink water was turning brown. That was our cue that the party was over for that summer escapade.

Out of these experiences, I became very mature even before I fully understood what responsibility really was. It wasn't always fun and games in those streets. I also saw another type of harmful game brewing with kids who were my age. Some of them got the memo to hustle in a different way. They slung dope, weed, and anything else they could get their hands on. There were some kids that learned to chase that fast money. That quick "easy" hit. Morning, noon, and night, you had the little hustlers on a block who were up to no good. You'd have to pass them on the way to school— seeing these little kids your own age moving "weight." Moving those little white dope-filled packets back and forth, from the corners to houses, like ants on a grid. Following the assembly line of movement, you'd see this older "boss dude," sitting on a porch down the block, orchestrating the whole transaction.

Navigating past these types of operations was tough. I would plead with my mother to not force me to run her errands because I hated passing by those dudes. She'd in turn warn me that she didn't want to see me around those no-good boys ever! Going past the older dude to get my mom her lottery tickets, he'd constantly try and recruit me to come work for him and make some "easy cash" as he put it. He'd casually lean on the porch stoop, saying, "When you gonna stop dreaming about your money when you can come here and get your money?" Even though I knew dudes were making money, I also knew that dudes were losing their lives as well. Needlessly wasting away in jail from doing that shit. I'm not going to lie, it scared the hell out of me. Life in my neighborhood was like a real-life *Invasion of the Body Snatchers* movie! When the boys would get together, they would always share cryptic stories about cats just disappearing off the block. "Yo, yo! Did you hear that Freddy's got twenty? Yeah, son. He won't be out 'til his daughter turns twenty-five!"

I tucked those stories away in my subconscious and said to myself, Daaaaamn! That sure as hell won't be me.

Dope dealing was never my thing. What I also learned by observation was that those in my neighborhood who did sling it were low-key ingenious brothers who didn't have the same positive structure in place that I did. The temptation was greater than their influence, I guess. These hustlers were the original businessmen that I grew up with. They knew about supply and demand like any other businessman. They controlled their product, recruited talented salespeople, and kept a firm grasp on their bottom line. The really good ones even knew about the

principles of horizontal distribution. They knew that smoking
their own product was bad for business because it ate into profits and fucked with your mind. I knew they were doing wrong,
but I still had mad respect for their ability to hustle.

Isn't that what being in business is all about? One dude in
particular that I would hang out with was my homeboy, Junior.
Growing up he was the best hustler on my block. Junior was
fly as hell because he was just cool, wise beyond his years, and
knew how to dress his behind off. Oh, and he always had a fine
Puerto Rican chick on his arm too! He never did well in school
and was always playing hooky. Junior was an only child who
basically lived by himself because his mom was never around,
so he essentially made his own damn rules. He could go and
come as he pleased and never had a curfew or nothing. When I
was twelve or thirteen, Junior was about four years older than
me, so age-wise he was someone I looked up to. Especially as a
young man just entering my teen years, it was cool to have one
of the slickest teenage cats as your friend—even if you knew
he wasn't doing right. Junior always said to me, "Yo, B man . . .
if you need anything, I got you. I got you, brother." I may not
have been the smartest kid, but I knew what "I got you" meant
and that it would come with some strings and shit. One of my
cousins used to make moves with Junior and I knew he got
locked up for doing some stuff.

Then one time I slipped and even entertained the thought
saying, "Okay. I'm about to hustle and get this money." Ironically, that was the same day the police came through our block
in full-force raid mode and shit. They cornered a bunch of
street kids in an apartment building and all I remember seeing
were my peers being led away in handcuffs, hands behind their
backs, and being put into the back of cop cars. It was traumatic!

Ah, hell no!

After that scene unfolded, I was like, "Nah, nah, we cool. I can't do that. I'm good. My mom and pops would trip too much." Junior didn't take that rejection to heart because unlike him, he knew I had to answer to my folks. For me, the drug game was a lesson in easy come, easy go. You could make a lot of money quickly, but just as fast somebody could roll up and take it from you. Everything you convinced yourself you were hustling for could be gone in one day. Correction . . . one minute actually if you were unlucky and got murdered in the streets. I knew I could make two or three grand a day, but then I might have to sit down for twelve years, lose all that momentum and lose all that money? Then, when I came out, I most likely wouldn't get no job because now I'd be a convicted felon? I did all that mental math and the risk-versus-reward ratio didn't pan out in my mind.

Junior got where I was coming from, and I respected where he was coming from. We respected each other's hustle and journey, but we also knew how to stay in our own lane and still be cool with each other.

* * *

My parent's antidote for keeping us out of trouble was to drill home the message that education was our ticket out. Driven by this notion, they scraped, saved, and sacrificed to make sure that my sister and I went to a private school. Everybody else on my block was going to the public school that was four blocks up the street and close by. Not us, we went to the private school that was ten blocks away, and we were forced to go past the public-school kids to get to our school. I remember the anxiety I felt because those public-school kids, my friends, would heckle us and call us sellouts the whole time we walked by. They especially clowned us because we wore our uniforms. Karen in her little blue plaid skirt and me in a shrunken blue tie with a corny-ass yellow shirt. We were not hard to miss at all. I always took off my tie, and we'd switch out our dress shoes for sneakers, in an attempt at disguising ourselves so we could try to blend in more. It was a lost cause because the neighborhood kids still knew where I was coming from. Nobody wore a corny button-down yellow shirt like that if they didn't have to. I wasn't fooling nobody! There was so much pressure to not look like an outsider in my hood. It determined how you were treated and received by the kids on the block. The tremendous burden to not be perceived as an outsider in your own community was real. I had to walk a fine line.

As an adult, I now realize my parents didn't have the extras to keep me in Nike, Adidas, and Fila, or donate to my swag game. They were too busy setting us up for the future. Keeping my sister and me in a private school must have been a Herculean task on a budget that was stretched to the brink. As kids, we mistakenly interpreted our regular no-name coats and no-name shoes as a form of lack. We didn't have anything fancy or flashy in our wardrobe. My mom would happily remind us, "I can't get you what you want, but I can get you what you need." My parents had their eyes focused on the prize, and I had my eyes set on the latest hyped-up Pumas! I thank God every day for giving me parents that were willing to sacrifice and abandon their own desires to provide the best they could for us. My sister and I were blessed with good ones.

When I was around thirteen my mom temporarily kicked my daddy out of the house. Just like that she had reached her

breaking point and told him to hit the road. This was traumatic for me because, despite the hard times, I always felt a
little inner boost of security and confidence in knowing that
my mom and dad were still married, together, and living in the
same house. For ninety-five percent of my friends, this was not
the scenario. I wore my family dynamics like it was a badge of
honor, something to be proud of. So, when Dad had to leave,
it rocked me to my core. I remember both of them sitting my
sister and me down at our kitchen table and Mom started out
by saying, "Right now things are tight and things just aren't
working out between Mommy and Daddy." My sister and I
went silent and started to blink wildly, looking back and forth
at them. "It's not your fault," she continued.

My dad chimed in and said, "Daddy's not going to be here
because Daddy's going to be gone for a while. Don't worry, I'm
going to come back and see y'all." After hearing the news, my
sister and I crumbled. I'll never forget that moment. We were
devastated! We were accustomed to not having much material
stuff, but at least we could count on the fact that we had an
intact family. That was our prize!

When it sunk in, we started screaming and hollering saying,
"Mommy, where's my daddy going? Where's my daddy going?"

My mom replied, "He goin' be alright. He goin' be alright.
He grown!" How the hell my dad being grown meant anything
to me as a child I have no idea. She continued, "And Momma
goin' be alright because Momma's grown too. Momma going
to do what's right for us!" That's the explanation she gave to
soothe us. There it was. We were sitting there stuck in the middle of a messy situation and all we knew was that two "grown
people" caused it.

Days after, we'd still break down crying periodically, "We

miss our daddy! We miss our daddy! When's Daddy coming back home, Mommy? When's Daddy coming back home?"

Like a real old-school Black Southern momma, this lady snapped and blacked out one day on us. She looked us dead in the eyes and yelled, "You ain't going to sit up here and keep crying for your daddy! We ain't going to sit here and keep talking 'bout your damn daddy. That's what we're not gonna do! If your daddy was doing what he was supposed to do, he wouldn't be gone! Now, you going get out my face with all that, and go to your damn room and do your homework! Your daddy WILL NOT be here today and that's all I'm goin' say about that! Now, FIX. YOUR. FACE!" Just like that, the tears dried up real quick and we officially shook. BOOM!

It was one of those times when your parents said something so mean and so blunt that all you could do was blink. Now that's a mic drop moment if I ever saw one. Her words landed just like an unexpected gut punch. Wham! It knocked the wind right out of us. Yo, it's cold, but it's true. I'd be up in my room crying to myself mumbling, "I miss my dad . . . I miss my dad!" It was clear we had no say in what was happening. She just reassured us that she was going to take care of us no matter what. She had been carrying us all along and had no intention of having shit fall off a cliff because Daddy was gone. That's the unquantifiable Black woman strength I grew up witnessing firsthand. What we wanted didn't matter because this was grown folk's business as they called it. We just had to find our own way to suck it up and deal. Them's the breaks, as the saying goes.

Don't get me wrong, times weren't always bad. One of my favorite childhood memories is the first time we all went to Atlantic City. I had never been to the beach before and I was psyched to go on a road trip. I'd seen a beautiful glimmering beach on TV, but now I was about to experience its beauty in person for myself. I was so excited! When we finally pulled up, I saw a little bitty amusement park roller coaster along the water. It looked like the best coaster in the world to me. I was salivating! I could have ridden that thing all damn day like I was riding the best, most thrilling ride at Six Flags.

This was also around the time when my parents had sprung for retainers from Dr. Freeman so that I could get my teeth right. I was on cloud nine all day, right up until I jumped into the raging ocean to swim, not thinking about my new expensive retainers. Frolicking carefree in the water, I opened up my mouth to let out a scream of delight. Before I had time to even react or close my damn mouth, my shiny new expensive grill flew straight out into the ocean. Oh my God! I was petrified. I had no idea how powerful the ocean was, or that it moved stuff with such force. When I came up to shore and told my mother, she stared me down like I was crazy and said, "Go back in that water and find it! Don't come out that water 'til you find it!"

Damn Momma, I thought to myself. You cold as fuck! I'm not sure if she knew how big that ocean was, but I went back anyway, to the exact spot I had lost them in. My eyes were burning as I blindly felt my way around in salty-ass water looking for those punk-ass retainers. It never dawned on me that there was no chance in hell I'd find them in the same spot where they bolted from my mouth. The ocean moves things, dummy! No retainers were found that day and my mother never let me forget it.

Even though I came from hard-working people, we were still always broke. I mean, we just never had anything extra left over for anything. Everything was always just enough. I played basketball, ran track, and played baseball growing up.

I always wanted to play football but was too damn skinny. Basketball was my main sport from grade school through to high school. I honestly thought I was going to the NBA, but then I never had anyone to take me to practices, or we never had any money to send me to camps. A little trivia for you: my cousin on my mom's side of the family is Shaquille O'Neal. Yep, Shaq Diesel. So, when I went off to college, I'd always hear the buzz around my young cousin Shaq. They'd buzz about him being a sure thing to go to the NBA. Shoot, at seven foot one, you better do something with all that height to get paid. Fuck, nobody in their wildest dreams expected him to dominate like he did, or become such a powerhouse entrepreneur, but we knew he was going places. We're all so damn proud of him and everything he's accomplished. Professional basketball just wasn't in the cards for me.

Seeing this constant struggle day in and day out made me realize I just didn't want that for my life when I got older. It was depressing. I was never able to get any little extra anything that I wanted because my parents just couldn't afford it. I always had to get the off-brand gear or something like it, but I never liked it. So, when I could earn my own money, I started working for myself and doing hustle moves. In my mind, I was like, I want to be able to buy what I want one day. I want to be able to go and buy something without looking at the tag one day. I want to go to high-end designer stores one day. I want to buy a nice car. I don't always want my cars to be used. It may sound superficial, but in reality, what my adolescent self was crying out for was greater than the material goods I was craving. I wanted to live a life of joy, success, and ultimately freedom from poverty. I wanted to create the financial space to be able to breathe. I craved freedom from the debilitating and limiting shackles of both mental and physical poverty.

I might have been about fourteen or fifteen when I finally reached my breaking point and shared this epiphany with my mom and dad. We were in the car driving somewhere and my folks were in the middle of a really heated conversation about money, as usual. It was the same fights they always had, and one my sister and I had heard thousands of times. "I can't pay for that. I don't have the money for this!" I was literally sitting in the back of the car and I could feel a claustrophobic sensation starting to take over my mind and body. Everything just had a feeling of being instantly pressurized in that car. Imagine seeing two people fighting constantly about the money they didn't have. I couldn't reconcile it because I saw how hard they worked. Out of nowhere, I don't know why, I just let out a guttural scream from the depths of my soul. Instantly, my father slammed on the brakes and I continued to scream, sob, and blurt out the words "I'm tired of it! I am tired of being poor. I don't want to be poor anymore. I don't want to live being poor. It's the worst! I can't do it anymore!" I continued screaming hysterically while my parents looked at me, frightened by what they were seeing. Feeling like I just had to get out and away from everything, I yanked open the car door and jumped out. I had a legit breakdown! My full-on Britney Spears moment! I continued to cry, "I'm gonna make it, Mom. I'm gonna make it! I can't do this anymore. I'm tired. I'm tired of not having anything that I want."

By this time my mother was completely bewildered and started crying herself. In between her own weeping she said, "Oh my God, you're embarrassed by us! We did everything we could. We tried . . . Oh my God, we tried! Hard as I work . . . I tried to do everything for you and it's still not enough!"

I didn't mean to hurt anybody's feelings. It was clear by her response that my momma and I were speaking different languages. I continued to scream, "I don't want to just be able to have that one thing that you can afford from Sears anymore. I can't have the shoes I want to look nice. I always have to look like, you know, like I got my stuff from the thrift store or something!" My anger, frustration, and exhaustion came pouring out of me like a raging river and I couldn't stop it. My chest was heaving up and down with each word and the tears continued to flow uncontrollably. My frustration bubbled over and consumed me in an inconsolable fit of rage. Quite frankly, I even scared myself.

After the outburst in the car, my parents were stunned into silence to see my raw emotion bubbling over and exposed. They knew their son and they knew I was pretty measured and not much of a crier. All they could say was, "Well how are you going to support yourself and where are you going to go?"

I answered, "I don't know where I'm going, but I'm getting out of here. I'm not gonna live in Newark for the rest of my life. I'm not gonna be around these people and this life anymore. I'm tired of it. I want to go somewhere where they got palm trees. I want to go somewhere where they got beaches. I want to see a different life." I finally said, "Ma, you ain't got to worry about me. You just take care of yourself. I'll be alright!" And just like that, I made my first life affirmation out loud.

* * *

I got my first real job at fifteen years old. I worked at the Newark Drive-In where all the cool kids hung out. Working to make pizzas, refill soda machines, and keep the popcorn machine going; you name it, I did it. Whenever there was a spill, I'd go in the back and get that mop to quickly clean it up. I was just like the Road Runner zipping around that old drive-in. After a while, I even earned the nickname Spill Bill.

I'll never forget the cashier lady with the big arms that worked there too. I was mesmerized by the slab of skin that would hang down whenever she'd reach across the counter to take people's money. She'd always come to work wearing her muumuu or housecoat or something flowy like that thinking it was concealing things. No matter what she was doing, especially when she rocked a short sleeve version, you could see the waddle waving at you. She would get on the microphone by the register and scream into it, notifying me that a spill happened somewhere by the machines. Groups of badass kids would pull the soda handle down too hard, spilling tons of sticky soda in a sudden whoosh onto the floor. I'd hear "arms" yell over the speaker, "B-I-L-L! There's a spill!" And like a racehorse hearing the bell, I'd set off to clean it up. I'll never forget those days!

One of my favorite things about the drive-in job was delivering food to people's cars during the movies. Many times, I'd walk up to the parked cars, and the windows would be all steamy and fogged up from couples making out. For a sixteen-year-old this was exciting. I'd stand there and stare for a few seconds trying to catch a glimpse of something I wasn't supposed to see. I was nosy as fuck! I'd say to myself, "Ooh, they in there doing it!"

It fascinated me because most people still believed in decorum. Then, they'd come up for air and catch me looking and say, "Hey! What you looking at?"

"Here's your pizza," I'd stammer in response, embarrassed

at being caught peeping. Later on, I would share the funny stories with my friends and we'd fall out laughing. Even though
I was exhausted after a long shift at the drive-in, smelling like
popcorn, melted butter, cotton candy, and pizza with a splash
of bleach, I knew deep down it was better than slinging dope
on the corner.

*   *   *

I'm not saying anyone would confuse Newark for New York
City, but in our 25.89 square mile city, we had some pretty big
culturally influential movements come through and take hold.
My city embraced the growing Black Panther movement of the
late 1960s and early 1970s. We went through the upheaval and
fear of the Newark riots in 1967, which left a very dark stain on
our town. It put a wedge between cops and the people they were
there to protect. In the riots, big scary military tanks invaded
our blocks and came down our streets creating fear and forcing
compliance. We had Black political activist Stokely Carmichael
come through to stage an uprising. We had the Honorable Elijah
Muhammad and the great Malcolm X and other Black Nation-
alists like Muhammad Ali influencing both the young and old
in Newark. On one hand, we knew we were poor, but on the
other, these Black cultural icons were teaching my community
about how powerful we could be if we united and supported
our own communities. They stressed that being self-sufficient
and self-reliant would put our destiny in our own hands. We
were culturally wealthy and had a lineage of excellence, but
continued to struggle economically because of the racism consuming America.

　　With that fire in our belly, the Black community of Newark

was powerful. With that knowledge, many of us put our passion into purpose and vowed to make more of ourselves than our current circumstances allowed. Approaching my graduation, I knew I was going to make something of myself. I already learned the importance of hustle from both my parents but in different ways.

My mom taught me the critical value of organized hustle. She believed in herself and found ways to make it all happen, even without a traditional educational pedigree. She bet on herself and pushed forward knowing she was bigger than her circumstances and bigger than her limitations. My dad taught me about a different hustle. He hustled with heart. Pops taught me that flexibility in your grind is just as important as being skilled. He was open to all possibilities that came his way and jumped on each of them with the same vigor and optimism each time. Each new job or side gig was a challenge and an opportunity to learn something new. He may not have gotten to his own promised land, but he helped me see mine even clearer.

The hustle I witnessed on the streets taught me to sharpen and trust my intuition, building my resilience. It taught me how to maneuver among all types of people and become a social chameleon. Understanding people's movements and motivations are vital to reaching success. The dudes on the street taught me how to bob, weave, and dodge to stay alive. They showed me the supply and demand game and how it applies to all products. I got that from the cats on the streets, and it has served me well every day since.

2

LIVE MIC

———

"MOVE THE CROWD"

Song by Eric B. & Rakim

I was definitely born to entertain. I didn't realize at first just how much this was true, but I knew I always loved to entertain my family, friends, and coworkers. Anytime I could bring a laugh or levity to a situation, I'd do it gladly. Making people feel good was my calling and I was damn good at it, if I do say so myself. It made me happy and ignited my soul to see people respond to what I delivered. To see the mental, physical, and emotional transformation that my simple words could bring about was exhilarating. I definitely had what I called my shit-talking moments. I knew I had a quick wit, allowing me to come up with the craziest one-liners that would have 'em rolling. Clowning in the school cafeteria or in my own cramped living room with my mom or family, I knew I had what it took to make people laugh. I was always the life of the party, but I never had the notion that it was possible to make a career out of it. It was just what I did. It was just how I was. When the college years came, I was psyched about exercising my independence and the prospect of getting out of my parents' house.

In my family, I had the distinction of being the first grand-kid to go to college and it was a big deal. Coming from parents who only made it to high school, and one who never completed it, my accomplishments were an extension of their unrealized educational dreams. Being first generational implants from the South, my parents' desire was to get a taste of a life that recognized them as human beings. They were slaying bigger demons so I didn't have to. Fighting the good fight in order to even exist and stay alive, they didn't have time to dream about that college stuff. Yet, they were still dreamers, and their unrealized dreams simmered like hot bubbling grits on the stove of frustrated ambitions. Labeled as what society classified as "uneducated," Moms and Pops took the pursuit of education very seriously. They had the dream for themselves, but sacrificed, labored, and secured it for their children. They wanted to see us do better than they ever did. I can hear my mother now. She would always say, "You are going to college, and you're gonna get educated. My name will go further than me!" For her it wasn't about the paper, it was about the promise. Her dreams drove my own ambitions. I carried that baton for the both of us.

College prep was an entire family mission. Ever since I could remember, my uncles and everybody in my family nicknamed me College. They used to say, "Hey, College! You better be ready, College. I want you to keep those grades up because you going to be the one to get out there, College!" Another uncle similarly labeled me Dollar Bill. He'd continually ask, "Dollar

Bill, hey, Dollar Bill! You ready for college, Dollar Bill?" Being destined for college was ground into my head at every turn. It wasn't up for discussion or debate; it was destiny. Basketball and sports were fine, but I was expected to go to college to learn some other shit too. It always burns me when I hear so-called scholars say Black parents didn't encourage education, or that there wasn't a strong focus in Black households on education. It's bullshit! Going to college was a primary topic of conversation for my folks; even though they had no idea how they would pay for it. It was the opportunity to remove those ceilings of limitations and secure a different legacy for us all.

Some of those limitations stifled plenty of African American males that I saw growing up in my neighborhood who didn't have an education or strong family guidance behind them. The defeated and lost ones who thought their only way to escape was getting that fast cash by slinging little plastic bags of poison at each other. It was about more than just pencils and books for me. It was life and death.

Finally, Rutgers University came calling. Like most college kids, I came in thinking it was all about nailing down my major. That golden ticket you're supposed to have all figured out when you are only eighteen or nineteen. The path that's supposedly going to set you up for the future. Well, I thought I did because I was going in focused and prepared. Initially, I did computer science because I thought I might be interested in writing codes and stuff like that. I was always kind of a closet geek because I loved computers. For a side hustle as a teen, I used to repair them and sometimes teach software classes to neighborhood folks.

Naturally, I thought I was going to harness that skill and make it my vocation. Reality check! After taking a few classes, the shit turned out to be so damn boring! It was just so one-dimensional and mechanical in the most intense way. I woke up one day and asked myself, Am I this motherfucking nerdy? For real! I don't want to do binary Xs, Os, and ones for the rest of my life. It was boring as hell and required having a solitary focus. It was the complete opposite of my extroverted person-ality. I affirmed to myself, This shit ain't cool! This shit here is for corn balls. I can't sit at a computer all day salivating over numbers and lusting after algorithms like they're a woman or something! I'm not that dude. I'm out! With that crossed off my career list, I went in search of another. I knew I still wanted to make lots of money at whatever I did. I always had suc-cess with little side gigs, so I switched my major to business. Looking back now, I guess you could say I dodged that damn pocket-protector-wearing bullet!

Alongside my business classes, I took African American Stud-ies, which was transformative. In these classes, I got my first for-mal understanding of the importance of Black culture throughout history, and the magnitude of our vital contributions. Growing up, like many kids my age, I went to schools that didn't teach us how amazingly invaluable Black people's inventions and input were to the creation of America. It wasn't just Black history, it created American history. Up until then, we only learned the American history that said, your Black guys were slaves. Hidden from us was the fact that Black people did big shit too. The sys-tem conveniently omitted that part of history. Becoming more educated and aware caused me to really dial in hard on Black pride and what my purpose was. I vowed to represent my family and Black men in a positive light in whatever I chose to do.

I knew Black men weren't monolithic thug-like creatures. I wasn't, and I knew a bunch of other dudes who weren't, so how come society perceived us all like that? Contrary to society's depictions, I knew as Black men we could be articulate, analytical, and resourceful. We could command any audience by squaring up and being super-savvy at work too. It was obvious to us that we could do other things besides playing basketball, throwing footballs, and pushing drugs in the ghetto. I just wanted to be a representation of the other lesser-reported attributes that Black men exuded. This was the filter I used to process all of my decisions. I promised myself that I would never lose sight of where I came from, the sacrifice it took, and what I overcame to get to college. It wasn't pretty. The struggle and decisions I made were deliberate. I wanted other dudes to look at me and say to themselves, "Yo, Bill Bellamy looks like me. He came from some rough spots like where I came from. If he made it, so can I! That's the dude to follow!"

I remained the same dude and went to the regular barbershop around the way. That was still a part of home for me. Growing up I played ball with the drug dealers but didn't sell dope. I hung out with grown-ass men soaking up their knowledge, swagger, and wisdom. I was quietly learning from their lives, soaking up the good parts of the game like a sponge. I knew where the easy money lived, but I was determined and clear-headed enough to know that it only brought short-term gain. I wasn't a short-term gain sort of dude. I had been conditioned to believe that education provided the long-term win and securing a career did as well. All throughout college, I knew drive and ambition had no ceilings. Those qualities came with no cap or limitations and that's what I wanted. I knew I was driven by the biggest of dreams. I let my dreams be my sails, fearlessly propelling me in the choices I made. I was determined to be focused and selfish with respect to my dreams.

I didn't let any distraction jump ahead of these ambitions. I was the captain of my own destiny.

One summer my mom got me an internship at Novartis, her pharmaceutical company where she had worked since I was a kid. They made all types of drugs and strong medication and stuff. I remember being on the plant floor and it would be crazy to experience the sights, sounds, and process of hundreds and thousands of plastic bottles shuffling down. Then, the capsules would make a swooshing sound as they'd drop into those bottles and swiftly move along the conveyor belts at lightning speed. After that step, the bottles were whisked off to be checked, sealed, and labeled. It was hypnotic and timed right down to the second. In that factory, everyone wore gauzy white hairnets and white gloves and hunched over the assembly line counting pills and making sure that everything was exact. That was quality control, the necessary grunt work required to deliver perfection. Checking and rechecking your work. One deviation, one hiccup, one interruption, and it could derail the whole operation, backing things up for hours. Isn't that how real life ran too? I was fascinated and drank it all in. All those packages, machines, and moving parts. Yeah, it was downright magic. I mean, I learned all types of different things and principles interning that summer and gained a new appreciation for the methodical steady work my mom did. I learned the beauty and value of process.

Coupled with that, I also hustled my way through college cutting hair and detailing people's cars. I was doing mobile car washing and detailing before that was even a thing. I would travel to the wealthy suburbs of New Jersey to pick up business with no more than a bucket, sponge, and some soap in hand. I went to where the money lived. I had all my shit ready

for self-promotion too. Just like a game show host, I would chat
it up, promoting my services to everyone who'd listen. Nobody
was off-limits to me. I had flyers printed and would rush door
to door handing them out. I had everything down to a system.
If you had two or three cars you wanted me to detail, I'd cut
you a break. One hundred and fifty bucks for two cars. There
were no fancy mobile detailing trucks back then so I'd have to
pray the client would let me use their hose and water. I would
scrub spilled shit on floor mats and pick at old gum. Spill Bill
reporting for duty! Clean inside spotlessly and wax on the outside just as meticulously. By the end of the day, everything
hurt. I mean my arms and shoulders would be on fire for a good
three days. That's what I learned from my dad. I mirrored his
"make it happen" mindset all throughout college to make sure
I kept money flowing into my pockets.

* * *

My official moment of clarity, when I acknowledged my desire
to become a stand-up comic, came in my sophomore year in
college. I was sitting in the College Ave cafeteria across the
table from my boy Jazzy, whose government name was Jeff
Combs. We were eating our burgers and fries, chopping it up
and talking shit back and forth to each other. Out of nowhere,
I stopped midsentence and looked over at him declaring, "Yo,
Jazzy! You know what? I'm gonna be a stand-up comedian."

He looked at me, paused, and started to nod his head slowly
in agreement, like he was finally catching the hook of a good
song. He responded, "Yo, B, I could see that. I could see that
shit. That shit would be a good look for you man. You funny as
hell! How you gonna do it?"

I said, "I don't know. I'm just gonna make 'em laugh and get paid!" Little did Jazzy know, I had just verbalized out loud, for the very first time, my life affirmation. And, for me, saying it to one of my boys made me accountable to it.

The fact that he didn't say, "Man, you're crazy," meant that he could see it too.

BILL BELLAMY INC. FORMULATING MY BRAND STRATEGY

I knew I had my hustle, my commitment, my funny, and my passion. I had me. I was my product. Growing up entwined with that "street life," I knew about supply and demand. In this case, I was the drug. I was going to get them drunk and high off of the laughs I was going to pull out of their souls. I was going to make people curl over in joy, with tears running down their face. I was going to get people hooked on my brand of funny.

I became the pusher.

One thing I knew right off the bat was I had to keep my nose clean and stay focused to be a success. McDonald's was a brand; Hershey's was a brand. I started to make the correlation that Bill Bellamy was the brand I needed to invest in. I would be like no other comedian out there. I'd create a demand for Bill and the only way they could get the product was to come through me. That's how I started looking at myself; just like a business entity.

I always say you can't talk about what you don't know about. I had a vision that I would be somebody—that I would do something big in life. After I vocalized my dream of being a comedian to my boy Jazzy, I knew it was time to see what else I could do.

The pilot light had been ignited and I needed some kindling for the fire. After all, vision without actions is just useless thoughts. In that spirit, I literally began doing gigs anywhere I could get on a stage and hold a live mic. I was hosting random karaoke nights and other bullshit. I was at the step show for the Omega Psi Phi and the Alphas. I was the go-to warm-up act for the musical bands that came to our school to perform. My goal was to just get myself in front of people to practice making them laugh. All different types of people too. I would take note of the types of things audiences laughed at and the types of things they gave me the side-eye for. I studied their body language; I studied the way they dressed. I paid attention to the demographic makeup of each group and played to each crowd differently. I made mental notes about what got the ladies turned all the way up and what got the fellas cranked. I also dissected what pissed them off too. I'd count how many laughs I got in each set and try to outdo myself each time. I became a full-time student of the craft. I respected the science behind it and was learning the algorithms of what made a successful comedian.

I wanted to be just like my idol Eddie Murphy. Coming up, in my generation of comics, Eddie Murphy was the first person that I saw that made comedy look fly. He was doing it in real time. This brother brought his own flavor of Kool-Aid to the party. You'd never see him wearing some buttoned-up regular corny suit on stage. He was a straight-up rock star with his own style of swag shit. He was showing the world that you could show up looking fly as hell, tell jokes, and motherfuckers would love you for it. He was the first dude I ever saw in my life wear a motherfucking pinkie ring over a glove. Now, stop and visualize that shit for a second. This Black motherfucker waltzed on stage to tell some jokes to other Black folk with a pinky ring o-v-e-r his glove! And, made the shit look fly! Oh, I see . . . Eddie's so fly that the pinkie ring belongs on top of the glove. Okay, cool, I can get with that.

I was never the leather pants nigga. I couldn't wear tight-ass leather pants on stage like Eddie because I was afraid of getting a yeast infection, or some shit like that. Nobody could match Eddie's natural swag. The women loved them some Eddie Murphy. He was the rock star influence that guided me. He was my alter ego when I stepped on stage. My personal style of comedic storytelling came from two different giants of comedy. I would say Richard Pryor and Bill Cosby influenced the storytelling aspect of my style the most. I remembered Bill could make anything sound funny. He would say something simple like, "And then this child came into the room. I looked him in the face and his mom said . . ." Yo, Bill didn't even have to finish the joke that shit was so brilliant. Funny just how he said it right out the box! Bill painted vivid mental pictures with words for his audience. He laid out details and transformed his vocals and face perfectly to match each story. He was a master storyteller.

Richard Pryor used his masterful wordplay to do the same thing. I remember Richard telling a joke once that went something like, "I shot the car. Then the cops came and then I said they don't shoot cars, they shoot nigg-cars." I was like, that shit is art . . . it's fire! His phrasing and inflections made his jokes priceless! It was a rhythmic dance of words. In their routines, they were known for bringing out a chair, sitting down center stage, and magnetically drawing the audience into them.

My zany, unpredictable off-the-cuff comedy style was definitely influenced by guys like Robin Williams. I just thought that Robin Williams must have been on some crack to do what he did and how he did it. He could do twenty voices within seconds of each other. He'd go from an old lady's voice to the heavily ethnic countryman, to another different type of lady's voice, to another man's voice, and never miss a beat. He was captivating to watch. He was so mesmerizing you couldn't look away. That's the unique and addictive product I wanted to deliver to my audiences. I said to myself, Yup, if I could have the stamina and energy of Robin Williams, the storytelling prowess of Bill Cosby and Richard Pryor, and the swag of Eddie Murphy, that's what Bill Bellamy's secret sauce would consist of!

Starting out, one of my biggest shows when I first started out was when I was a contestant in the Delta Sigma Theta male pageant. It was crazy because all I kept saying to myself was, My God, I ain't got no talent to showcase. I mean the other dudes in the pageant were ready! Dudes had all sorts of talents: magicians, singers, poets, all with accompanying elaborate props and shit. They were riding unicycles, reading original soul-searching poems, and doing magic tricks and all this other goofy shit. I was like, Man, I'm gonna see what I can pull off. I'm gonna try to win this cool six-hundred-dollar prize right here! Tell you what else I'm gonna do, I'll just tell a few jokes. Bam! That's all I did for my measly four-minute talent segment. I told some jokes.

I was funny as hell.

Afterward, all I could hear were the girls on campus laughing and flirting coyly with me, saying, "Ooh, that Bill's so damn funny!" They would say that rubbing their hand across their upper chest; that's how you knew they were feeling you. "He's so crazy! Ooh, Bill, you stupid as fuck!" Translated into street slang . . . Ooh boy, you could get it! They loved me, and more importantly, they were taking notice of my style and talent. I would smile to myself when I heard them because I knew that if nothing else, I had the women hooked. They liked my chocolaty brown skin, disarming charm, and quick wit. I made a point of consistently flattering the ladies in the audience and leaving them feeling good about themselves. I would build them up and show them maximum love and mad respect. It was a really simple formula. Oh yeah, you know I won that little Delta Sigma Theta male pageant shit that year and walked away with the six hundred dollars.

While thinking of how and where to get my practice doing stand-up gigs, I was diving deeper into courses on finance and marketing at school. I was always intrigued by money, numbers, and the mechanics around making stuff sell and marketable. Economics classes, tracking how money worked, supply and demand, gross national product, and stuff like that. I soaked in information about monetary funds and how money flowed throughout the world markets. It started the wheels spinning. I thought that I was going to have a good solid financial education to take the business world by storm. My mind was still firmly rooted in the pursuit of attaining a good education. Religiously I heard my mom and dad's words urging me to get a good job and make a success of myself through education. All this learning I was doing unwittingly opened my mind up to the potential of Bill Bellamy as a brand and not just a one-dimensional performer.

First, I knew my product had to be reliable. Second, it had to do something unique. I decided my brand was going to be consistent in making people feel good. Making people forget their own problems, even if it was only for a few minutes. Third, my brand had to be clean so it could stay marketable to everyone. You've never heard of McDonald's, Burger King's, or

Coca-Cola's name mixed up in no sideways messy shit! They don't mess with the brand ever; that's the holy grail. The goal was to stay as far away from trouble, and people who were nothing but, at all costs. There would be no derailments, train wrecks, or forced errors during these learning years. I was here to soak up as much as I could, make some side cash, and get the hell out to make some real money.

I was determined. I was about to hustle this game, just like a dope dealer. The difference was where I was going to deliver my goods. I was always calculating the potential and odds behind every move I made. What's the strategy for this play? What would happen if I did this? I was constantly contemplating my next move. That's the pedigree I came from. My parents might not have had a boatload of assets to give me, but they equipped me with the best asset of all. They taught me how to survive, hustle, and make something out of nothing. They showed me how to reinvent myself. All of this while keeping my integrity uncompromised and intact.

I remember this major step show I opened up for while in college. This shit was the talk of the campus; it was a big deal. The Qs won that night and I was scheduled to do an opening stand-up routine there. This dude named Steve, a Sigma cat who took the stage right before me, got booed mercilessly off the stage and this put me on edge. It was embarrassing as hell because it happened in front of about six thousand people. Adding to the insult, the crowd threw pennies at his ass to get him off stage. Following directly behind him, I mumbled to myself, Oh shit, I cannot get booed in front of my friends! I knew I had to do some fly shit; something spectacular. I recruited about five of my boys to be my hype men when I took the stage. The plan was to make our entrance in a diamond formation, with me in the middle, to Eric B. and Rakim's song "Move the Crowd." I stood in the center of them and when we hit our mark my boys dispersed, leaving me standing solo in the middle with the spotlight on me. It was lit! The crowd went bat shit! The women were losing their minds screaming! I mean losing it. I made a name for myself that night and definitely had people buzzing. That's when I first realized how packaging your shit right, even as a comedian, had a profound impact on the reaction you got. Now that's real-life marketing right there.

Another huge boost early in my comedy pursuit came from my girl, singer Regina Belle, who also went to Rutgers University. Although she was three years ahead of me, she looked out for me big time. Regina could sing her behind off, and she was doing really well on the music scene. One year she came back to campus to do a huge performance. Remarkably, she let me open the show. This was an unheard-of break because my ass was still in college and she was already blowing up music charts. I came off so nice that night that when I graduated from school, Regina Belle asked me to go on the road and be her emcee and opening act! I mean she was touring with the O'Jays at the time. The fucking O'Jays—are you kidding me? You know them? "You're my darlin', darlin', baby . . . " You were raised under a rock, in the deepest part of the ocean, if you don't know the rest of the hook to that song! I was star-struck. I said to myself, Damn, Bill, you're out here fucking with real stars. We are in the game! It was a crazy head trip and a huge blessing.

I remember Mr. Eddie Levert, one of the O'Jays, used to guide me, "Yo, man, you got something special going on. Now I'll tell you what now. You got 15 minutes upfront, and you may have four or five in between. And, if I do this," he said as he motioned, stretching his hand wide in a back-and-forth motion, "that means s-t-r-e-t-c-h. Meaning you got a little more time." I was learning the ropes of taking my shit to a prime-time big stage. This experience solidified for me that I belonged there; I had something special.

It was transformational.

Even though I was killing it with comedy and doing major gigs, I was still of the mindset that I had to get a regular job. After all, that's what my parents sacrificed and sent me to school to do. To get a good education, a great job, and make something of myself. That's what we were taught in those days. Thinking outside of the box career-wise was still a fringe concept. We weren't raised to be athletes, ballers, musicians, or comedians. They were considered hobbies and "cute" side hustles. So. After I graduated from college, I got a "real job." A really big job.

* * *

My first adult job was as a marketing manager at Leggett & Myers, a tobacco company. No, I didn't smoke but somehow my job was to try to figure out how to get young people to think smoking was cool enough to buy our products. Don't judge a motherfucker decades later! It was a whole different era, and a very different time.

I got the job through my friend's dad, Mr. Hensley. I grew up knowing that Mr. Hensley was a successful corporate businessman. Back then, not many Black men reached such a level of mainstream corporate success. Mr. Hensley was definitely that Black unicorn type of figure for me. He had some real clout at that white company. He was the only Black guy at that level who had the power to bring in someone who looked like him. He saw how I moved with the ability to turn it on and off, playing the crowd-pleaser game seamlessly. Over the years I had built great customer service skills and was able to converse with all types of people at all levels. I was a natural-born salesman and this was a valuable skill. Mr. Hensley noticed my work ethic and hustle during my college days, doing all my various gigs and side gigs detailing rich people's cars on the weekends and outside of downtown stores while they shopped for the afternoon. One day he said to me, "You're a hustler, young man! Bill, you started your own business. I like that you're a go-getter. When you get out of college, you call me and I may have an opportunity for you." What made that statement even more remarkable was that this man was treating me like I was his own son by taking me under his wing. I did not take him, or his belief in me, for granted. I would make him proud if I ever got the opportunity.

Straight out of college, not straight out of Compton, I had a staff of five people working under me, a company car, an expense account, and a bigger salary than anyone I knew. Thirty thousand dollars a year to be exact. That was a whole lot of money back in the 1980s, especially for someone so young with no family obligations. It was a good life. So, I was done, right? I had technically made it. During this time, I was also moonlighting at night doing comedy while trying to hold down a demanding professional life from 9 to 5. Juggling all this shit was tougher than I thought. I would go straight from the office to perform at open mics. Everyone knew me for dressing really fresh and fully suited up. They'd say, "Bill Bellamy, he is so fresh!" Little did they know I was always in a suit because

I was coming straight from my day job. I had such a love for comedy, the stage, and the people that I almost broke my neck trying to make it all work at once. The problem was that my day job didn't magically end when five o'clock hit. At the management level, it required late-night meetings, and overtime too. It caused major conflicts and I couldn't get out to comedy gigs enough to make a major impression or connections. I was too preoccupied with juggling day-to-day meetings and paperwork from my office life.

Almost two years into my role at Leggett & Myers, I was being groomed for an even bigger role. The company wanted me to go back to school to get my MBA, and they even committed to pay for it. Shit, now that's a come-up. I was one of only a few Black sales guys and I was going places. I was on the trajectory to the top. At this point, I felt like I was at a crossroads in my life. I had a solid opportunity to remain at this desk job, a traditional corporate path, slowly being engulfed in a sea of responsibility and never making it out to comedy shows. After all, it's what I went to college for and it was a promising job for sure. Sure, I'd be climbing the corporate ladder and it didn't appear like there was a ceiling on how much success I could have there. But was that the success I really craved? If I stayed on this path, ultimately my opportunities would always be defined by other people.

And yet, this was a proven roadmap for "success" that most people followed. This was the American way. What if I wanted to create my own path and a new definition of success? I had already made the promise that there would be no glass ceilings on my success if I bet on myself. I was in the business of Bill Bellamy. I wanted to do comedy more than anything. I knew that; I believed it with every fiber of my soul. It didn't matter how long it took either. If I left the security of a traditionally great job, I wouldn't be losing because I would be gaining my independence again. I would be taking a bet on me. The incident that solidified my decision was when I was out on a routine sales call with my boss.

Once or twice a month Mike Rossi, my regional manager, would review my accounts. He'd take me out to lunch and we'd go over sales numbers vs. projections and go through current or upcoming promotions for the region of the supermarket and other retail accounts I managed. During this one particular visit, as we were driving back in the company car, Mike turned to me and said, "So, Bill, where do you see yourself going? What type of lifestyle and home do you see yourself living in within the next few years?"

I replied, "Well, Mike, I see myself living in a house like that." I pointed to this big old sprawling two-story mansion in one of the wealthy New Jersey suburbs we were driving through. "That's it. Yeah, that's the house right there."

He looked at me stunned. He said, "That house?" His eyes were all bugged out and shit. "I don't even live in a house like that!" he spat out, shocked by my audacity.

I said, "Oh, okay. Well, you asked me what type of lifestyle I saw for myself and what type of house I saw myself in. So, I said that's the kind of house I want to live in one day." I really wanted to add motherfucker at the end of my response, but I held my tongue.

"Woooooooow!" he added in a drawn-out sign of disbelief. "I don't know if you can live in a house like that working for this company."

It was at that very minute that my inner voice screamed

loud and clear, Oh well, I guess I won't be working for this company! Simple and clear, that's what it said.

Carrying around my unsigned resignation letter in my briefcase for weeks, I was so nervous to fully commit to that inner voice. Until I could muster up the balls, the letter just sat there in the back of my briefcase collecting dust. One day, Mr. Rossi asked me to come to his office. When I arrived he started his corporate speech, "Bill, you're doing a great job. You're excelling fantastically. You're a young African American guy in the right place at the right time. I'm going to put you in a position to go back to school for your MBA. You can come back in eighteen months and your salary will increase from thirty thousand dollars a year to one hundred and fifty thousand a year." Remember, I was still only twenty-two years old at the time. "You'll be making more money than me soon and you're going to be the first African American man to do this at the company. You'll be in charge of this whole team!"

His voice trailed off, becoming inaudible because all I could hear were my thoughts, getting louder and louder in my head. My inner voice started to scream, My life will be OVER if I take this job. I think I've got meetings and paperwork now? I'll never be able to do comedy. I'll be chained to a desk, or traveling to corporate meetings and conferences and all that bullshit. I'll work for someone else for the rest of my life. I won't be able to do shit. Without even being conscious of my real-time reactions, I reached my hand into the back of my briefcase and pulled out my resignation letter. Extending the paper in his direction, I handed him the now-signed letter I had prewritten. I started my speech, "Sir, I'm sorry, but I can't do it. Sir, I wasn't going to do this today, but . . ." I went silent and got the impression I didn't need to say anymore. I knew it was an amazing, possibly once-in-a-lifetime type of opportunity, but at that moment I knew that I had to turn it down if I was ever going to go after my dreams. Right then and there I cut the umbilical cord that was feeding me very well and decided to fly, or flop, on my own with absolutely no safety net. I took the final leap into the unknown and bet on myself!

Even though I left my cushy corporate job, I realize to this day that without Mr. Hensley there would be no Bill Bellamy. He took me under his wing and made my dreams come true, even if it wasn't the dream I chased. In a lot of ways, early on he gave me exactly what I thought I wanted and what I thought I needed to be a success. When I got the dream career, I very quickly realized that this was not the shoe that fit best. I could have spent decades learning that lesson. I could have spent a lifetime chasing the wrong dream, missing out on my true calling. Without that job early on, I'd probably be living someone else's life, chasing someone else's dream. Thank you, Mr. Hensley!

I knew I needed to float for a while, without too many commitments, so that I could figure my life out. It's terrifying and electrifying to decide to pursue your dreams, and I was about to find this out firsthand. At this point, I was completely fueled by the fire in my belly, and I was about to overfeed that son of a bitch!

3

IT STARTED WITH A BOOTY CALL

"BOOTI CALL"
Song by BLACKstreet

What I did next was purely survival instinct. I paid my rent for the next six months, put some money in the bank, and told my family and friends I quit my job to pursue comedy full time. Then, when the news circulated, the barrage of questions came flooding in. "You did WHAT? How are you going to pay rent? You don't have an agent! How will you get booked? You don't even have a manager! What about your company car? You don't even have a car!"

I had all their questions answered as well as I could at that point. What I didn't have figured out was my transportation situation. I didn't want the job, but I sure missed that free car! Soon after, I got my own Honda Accord and kept it pushing.

Finally, free from a desk job, I started to really get bubbling on the comedy circuit. I was doing gigs in the tristate area—New Jersey, New York, and Connecticut. There were no popping comedy clubs in New Jersey, so the goal was to get discovered in New York City. One of the most popular TV shows at the time was *Showtime at the Apollo*. It was a talent show which came on every Friday night and everyone watched it. They had a popular amateur night which gave national exposure to undiscovered talent. This was a huge deal and a coveted opportunity for anyone who wanted to be anyone in Hollywood. I set my sights on this opportunity. I had to get on that show. The host was Sinbad at the time, a funny, goofy, and charismatic light-skinned comedian, who always kept the audience in stitches. When I finally got the opportunity to appear, I'll never forget that on that particular evening everyone got booed off the stage! Even some of the professional acts. Just my fucking luck! I got the crowd with the mean motherfuckers who must have skipped breakfast, lunch, and dinner that day. The pissed-off crowd. In retrospect it was motivational, making me even more focused on killing it when I got my turn, I was determined not to fail. Hell, my mother was in the audience. I couldn't get booed in front of my mamma!

When my turn came, I went balls to the wall! I went absolutely ham! So many stars had touched that stage; it was a rite of passage for artists, but it was intimidating as hell. I wasn't wearing leather pants like Eddie, but I sure as hell felt my nuts about to slide down my legs with all the sweating I was doing. I puffed out my chest, rubbed the "Tree of Hope" good luck talisman offstage, and stepped out under the blazing theater lights to throw all my best shit out there. Don't you know it, from the same salty-ass crowd I actually got a standing ovation! A goddamn standing ovation! I'll never forget that feeling. It was a resounding confirmation that I was on the right path. My true ordained path. After that night, my confidence soared like a motherfucker. My name began to make noise in the Big Apple and it felt so good! I was on a roll, baby!

You never know what will happen in your life unless you try. I've often been a risk-taker and was now starting to get the recognition I knew I could get if I devoted the time to the craft. The greater the risk, the greater the reward—I've lived my life knowing this. My next break would come in 1991. That's when I met Bob Sumner, who was a Jersey native and a serious connector. He knew everybody. He also knew about a new show in the works at HBO that would later be known as *Def Comedy Jam*. There was a nationwide comedy search underway, and they were looking for the funniest up-and-coming comedians in the country. Bob would ironically end up being the talent coordinator for the show. And, that's how fate stepped in! Life can be so awesome when all the stars line up. This perfect alignment led to my biggest opportunity.

Back in the day, there was a comedy club in Harlem called Uptown Comedy Club. New York's hottest up-and-coming comedians all hit that stage and entertainment executives littered the audience. I'd written down a new joke concept called "Booty Call" and was planning to drop it on the audience there. I had gotten the idea for the set from a story I read in the newspaper. To show you how off the cuff it was, I originally wrote the damn joke on a paper towel. Back then, I didn't have a recorder or anything like that to save jokes and phrases that popped into my head throughout the day, so I'd write on anything I could grab and shove it in my pocket. I didn't realize it then, but that little "Booty Call" reference I stuffed in my pocket would change my career and life forever.

One evening I drove into New York to finally take my stab at bringing my brand of funny to the Uptown Comedy Club. For the life of me, I could not find any parking, which was typical of Harlem. Running out of time, I took my chances and double-parked my Honda. While in the club I kept praying to Jesus that I wouldn't get towed. The club was owned by two brothers, Andre and Kevin Brown, who agreed to let me do a set that night. I was pumped! When it was about to be my turn, I went up to the steps leading to the stage to wait until Charlie Burnett was done with his set. At that time, Charlie was probably one of the most prolific street comedians in all of New York. Back in the day, he should have rightly gotten a gig on *Saturday Night Live*, but I don't know why that never went down. He was bar none one of the most hilarious and powerful comics on the scene. Period. While I was waiting for my turn, I was also surveying the audience's reactions. People were doubling over laughing; drinks were spilling. He was that level of funny. Charlie really knew how to bring the house down. As this was all playing out, I was still patiently waiting off to the side. Just as I was standing there, the owner Andre came around the corner and said to me, "Yo, B man, you know, Charlie's killing right now. You know what I'm saying? I don't think you should go on tonight. You can come back next week."

I was like, "Yo, Dre! Yo! Nah, nah. I can't do that." I'm not going to lie, that shit pissed me off.

"No disrespect, B. I don't want to put you through that. I love you man, but I can't let you go on tonight because it's just ridiculous. Look at Charlie killing, right now!" Andre continued.

"Nah, it don't matter, bro. It don't matter if Jesus is up there on that stage, bro. Let me go on. I've come too far to turn back now. You never know who's in the building in this game!" This is why you *must* always follow your gut and instincts in life.

"Alright! Alright! Go out there then. Take the mic and get killed," Dre said, a little ticked off by my decision.

I thought to myself, You know what I'm gonna do? I'll start with my closing set. I had a joke that I knew was smokin' hot. I'll start with my closer, work backward, and then throw my new "Booty Call" thing in the middle. Then, I'll close on another joke because I didn't know if "Booty Call" was going to work or not.

Where did this Booty Call concept come from? It came out of two situations I witnessed playing out in pop culture and across the front page of newspapers. I conjured up the idea during the time of controversy for boxer Mike Tyson. He found himself convicted of sexually assaulting a young lady he invited to his hotel room late one night. Not that there was any humor in the situation, but there were thoughtful questions that surfaced. Concerns about making sure women didn't leave themselves vulnerable, or in harm's way, during certain situations.

Secondly, the concept was inspired by navigating the challenges of dating at that time. The scenario that I wrote reflected on a typical Friday night for a twenty-something-year-old man. I was setting up a situation where he had a few dollars in his pocket, accompanied by a flashy new apartment of his own. Basically, he's the type of guy who was ready to show the world he had arrived. Obviously, when I wrote the joke, there was no Tinder, Bumble, Match.com, Instagram, or Facebook, and definitely no swiping to the damn right or left. It was the

1990s, all we had were our little black books, Rolodex, and flavored condoms.

During my brainstorming session, I said to myself, How can I make all these factors funny while explaining what's going on in dating culture? Out of nowhere, the words "booty" (because what man doesn't think about it 24-7), and "call" just popped into my head. I put them together and the light bulb went off instantly for me. The phrase was simple, catchy, funny, and user-friendly. It explained the essence of what guys were doing when they called up girls in the wee hours of the morning inviting them to come over. They were phoning it in. They were dialing up that booty! I created a descriptive label for what was already happening. Genius branding, if I do say so myself. Who knew? Booty Call was also a phrase that wasn't offensive and something that could be said on TV. That's another reason why I came up with it. Now if I had only trademarked it back then, I'd be retired today with money pouring out of every crevice! Do you know how many Booty Call checks I should have collected by now? Shhhhiiiit!

Cut to it—I go on that stage that night at Uptown Comedy Club and started with my closer as planned. Boom! I got 'em! The girls were going crazy. The dudes were laughing, but trying to be extra cool with it. I hit them with another good joke. Bam! The place went off. Now I was at the point where I was riding the Charlie Barnett wave. Finally it was time to go for the jugular. I threw the "Booty Call" reference in the mix and the crowd lost their shit! It was the first time I ever told that joke and it landed perfectly. Based on the reaction of the crowd, I knew that I had found a good thing. I knew that there was nothing else to talk about. The end. As soon as I came off stage, all these HBO people met me on the other side with nothing but love.

I taped *Def Comedy Jam* in October and it aired in January 1992. I was the first comedian on the first airing of *Def Comedy Jam*. You could say I popped their cherry! Being the first meant that I benefited from being featured in all those promotional releases leading up to the show's launch. My face was on the TV on repeat. Every time you saw the trailer for *Def Comedy Jam*, you saw me. It forced people to take notice and think to themselves, Who's this new dude right here? I couldn't have planned it better if I tried.

Looking back at it now, it amazes me because I was actually making a damn good life for myself. Bill Bellamy Inc. was doing stuff. Big stuff. Meanwhile, I got a reoccurring gig hosting an R&B showcase in New York City called "R&B Live," set up by Bob Sumner. I told you he was a godsend in my life. He told me about a spot where they were doing music and other acts. I hosted the show during the time when producer Jermaine Dupri had just launched a brand-new label called SO SO Def Records. He had compiled an impressive roster of young artists like Xscape, Bow Wow, and Kris Kross. One night Jermaine was showcasing Kris Kross. During that evening I remember skeptically remarking to Jermaine, "Yo, my man, what's the name of your group? Kris Kross? Is it really Kris Kross? And, they have on backward clothes? What is wrong with these young kids? They done lost their damn minds!" Can you believe they went on stage and the song they did that night was "Jump": "The Mac Dad'll make ya (jump, jump). The Daddy Mac'll make ya (jump, jump)." I said, Oh, shit! Those little kids had everybody bouncin' in the club! They shut my skeptical ass all the way up. FYI, they would go on to be huge stars. Take that, Bill Bellamy!

As the night was winding down, Bob Sumner and I were standing around chatting and a lady named Tracey Jordan made her way over to me nonchalantly and said, "Hello. Oh my God, you were really funny tonight. You're really a good host."

I said the usual pleasantries, "Aww, thank you, thank you, I really appreciate it." Then Bob, who made the official introduction, pulled me a little closer to him, leaned in, and whispered, "You got to keep in touch with her." I had no idea she was a talent executive at MTV Networks.

A few days later, Tracey made contact with me and said she wanted to see me do my stand-up routine again. I realized that this was a huge development. People in her position didn't reach out just because. I was beyond psyched and definitely on my A-game! She traveled to the Boston Comedy Club in Boston, Massachusetts. I was doing a showcase gig there that Barry Katz, who owned the Club at this time, invited me to. Barry informed me that MTV was looking for new VJs for their network. I didn't even know what the hell a VJ was, but I knew I wanted to be one. Shit, I didn't even have MTV at that time.

That showcase gig gave Tracey another view into the depth of my comedy outside of just hosting a show. She got to experience me doing stand-up. Doing my thing. After the show, she reached into her bag and pulled out her business card. Sure enough, it said MTV on the small white card in the bold primary yellow and red colors. My set and style must have left a great impression because she quickly gave me an opportunity for an audition with MTV. Mind you, at the time, I was doing all of this networking by myself. I didn't have a manager or agent. What I did have was my roommate, Ronald Workman, who I coaxed into pretending he was my manager. In true high school fashion, I convinced him to crank call the number on Tracey's card. I was like, "Yo, act like you're my manager. Call this number and see if it's real." Being the good hype man and supporting castmate, he called the number. Yep, it was real. It was MTV Networks! We were like giddy schoolgirls. We were cracking up, repeating, Oh, shit! It's real! I ended up going into MTV's offices and did what they called a screen test. The next thing I knew, I got a thirteen-week trial with MTV. I was officially in the game and rolling uphill now! The rest was history. This is how I got to be a part of the MTV family! The road to get there was straight-up grind, sprinkled with a whole lot of God!

It's still surreal to think that only a few short months after saying so long to my corporate path, I met the HBO executives who got me on *Def Comedy Jam*. Oh, and I was on MTV by the time I was twenty-four.

I knew in my spirit I wasn't ever meant to be some corporate dude. I was meant to be the captain of my own ship and excel at the business of Bill Bellamy. None of it would have happened if I didn't take that bet on myself . . . There are no coincidences. Ever!

4

TUNED IN AND TURNT UP—MTV DAZE

"STARTED FROM THE BOTTOM"

Song by Drake

Early in my entertainment career, one of my mom's biggest fears was that I would go to Hollywood, become indoctrinated, and get strung out on drugs. Through her limited exposure to that world, that was the inevitable fate, that's what you did. You lost your soul and yourself when you hit the big time. I said to her, "Mom, I'm not going to do drugs."

"Well, you be careful, Bill, because that's what they do out in Hollywood. They do drugs and they do cocaine, and they do other stuff. Then you gonna be strung out in the middle of the streets!"

"I'm not gonna do drugs. I'm not going to be a drug addict,"
I insisted. "They got money out there and I'm gonna find out
how to get it. That's my drug!"

A big part of how I got where I did in my life was choos-
ing to bet on myself. No one thought I could make it as a
comedian—not my family, not my friends. They wanted me to
stay in my traditional job, going with the safe bet, but I knew it
was slowly sucking the life out of me. I chose to not let the fear
of failure, or my mom's irrational fear of me becoming a drug
addict, hold me back. If you don't believe in yourself in this
life, you'll always stay confined in a box. A box not of your
own construction either. Never thinking of what more could be
possible if you just stepped out on faith. I can't stress enough
that you must believe in you!

*   *   *

I officially had my worldwide debut on *Def Comedy Jam* in January 1992. Then debuted on MTV a few short months later in April
1992. It literally looked like I blew up overnight because I was
on *Def Jam* HBO over here and two seconds later, you saw me
on another major station, MTV, over there. To add to the colos-
sal impact, both shows catered to two totally different audience
demographics. One network was strictly urban and culturally diverse and the other was more Wonder Bread, all-American, and
mainstream. In a nutshell, more white people, and more suburban
America. Cornering both these markets in a relatively short space
of time gave the perception that I shot straight out of a rocket. It
appeared like all this success just happened, like a magic trick—
poof! Nobody saw the struggle behind this "instant" success
story.

When I started at MTV, I was supposed to be an in-studio personality. As a VJ, which was short for video jockey, I was never cast to interview the most iconic names in music. My agreed contract was to feed out the popular music of the day to the people. Plain, simple, cut, and dried. At the outset, my first show was originally called *Fade to Black*. Ironically Al B. Sure was the host at the time. My role was to blend in and disappear, allowing the music to shine through. Just a facilitator. The executives at MTV looked to the Billboard charts to tell them what was trending, in demand, and ultimately what should be featured. Those charts were their bible and in the 1990s they were MTV's equivalent of today's Google algorithm: what's popular becomes more popular until you're inundated with it. Effectively squeezing out anything new, different, or smaller. Repetition became reality, but that's not always the best barometer of what people around the country were actually listening to. It really only captured a small sampling of an even smaller sector of music listeners. There were many flaws and cracks in that system.

In those days, and even somewhat today, the world of MTV was so insulated, mysterious, and extremely glamorous. Once you got your exclusive membership, it was up to you to orchestrate your journey and experiences. This was right up my alley. I was used to having to figure shit out on my own. Accustomed to learning through observation, finding the rhythm, and jumping in the middle like an intense Double Dutch session. Little did we all know, in a way, the 1990s were the final age of uncontrived innocence. It was the last decade before the internet revolution. After the internet hit, everybody's shit would be busted open, up for grabs, and seamlessly shared across an unimaginable number of outlets and platforms. We weren't ready.

My first days at MTV felt like I was working on a college

campus again with a lot of young creators. Tons of young people were coming out from every corner of the building. There was an electricity that vibrated throughout the office. People were buzzing and frolicking around everywhere, laughing, running, and being youthful. Young people could be seen and heard playing background music in their equally portioned cubicles, humming along and bobbing their heads while they worked. Bold, contrasting loud colors decorated every wall in the studio. If it screamed youthful and hot, our studios oozed it.

Demographically, there were predominantly white kids that worked in our office. Only a few of the staff were Black and even fewer were in positions of power, or decision-making roles. The Black creatives that were there made a big impact and contribution to Black music culture. Tracey Jordan, the woman who brought me to MTV, was the head of talent and relations; she was Black. A couple of really cool Black producers were doing big things, like Jack Bennett, the producer of *Yo! MTV Raps*, and Penny McDonald, my producer on *MTV Jams*. I also had a friend named Eugene Caldwell who worked in production.

Every office at 1515 Broadway had a television on with MTV flashing live images from whatever show was airing. That bright pink sticker logo was plastered everywhere you looked. It reinforced the carefree lifestyle sentiment the brand oozed. Cameras were everywhere too; they were shooting all different types of things at all different angles. It was damn near like living in a fishbowl. I've never experienced anything like it. I worked at their national studio location, which converted to virtually any set at the drop of a dime. I called it the Transformers set. We could seamlessly transition a set from *MTV Jams* to *Yo! MTV Raps* to *Top 20 Countdown*, with full branding elements and flair represented for each. It was fascinating, especially for someone whose only experience with set decoration was adding a stool on stage to do a routine. That's it, no-frills. When the crew was done setting the room, you'd swear that you had gone to another building and switched spaces entirely. They were so clever and resourceful with it.

Initially I was hired to host a daily two-hour music show called *MTV Jams*. The lively multi-format show was created to bridge the gap between rap music and top 40 R&B music. The network's powers that be were starting to realize that "Black" music came in different forms and catered to many different audiences, just like other white artists did. My show was the "link program" that wasn't just totally dedicated to hip-hop. It was the brainchild of Tracey Jordan and Penny McDonald. They recognized the lucrative gap in their coverage. The goal was to grab audiences in love with Brian McKnight, Vanessa Williams, Toni Braxton, SWV, Jade, and H-Town type of music. These types of artists would've never seen any play whatsoever on *Yo! MTV Raps*. They were outside the show's DNA, so naturally, they flocked to me and my show. If it was a hip-hop song that was in the top 20s or a top 40s trending song, it had a green light to be played on *MTV Jams*. If it wasn't, it was considered an underground song and would probably get no love, or it would probably stay on *Yo! MTV Raps*.

Even though this was the internal division as to where music was played and promoted, music legends like Nas, Diddy, Jay-Z, Biggie Smalls, Tupac, and Ice Cube blew up partly because of *MTV Jams*. Their songs got way more airplay on my show because it came on more frequently than *Yo! MTV Raps* did. *MTV Jams* inevitably became a lynchpin in the making of music's super artists because it allowed me to showcase them as multidimensional people. Viewers got to really know artists and become invested in who they were as people and the struggle behind their successes. In many ways it was easy for me because this was my own story; therefore it felt organic and comfortable. I was given the opportunity to shine a light on the struggle behind the glitz. It gave me great pride to be the truth-teller . . . the revealer. I had the bandwidth and airtime to introduce the audience to the flavor behind the music.

It was powerful to have daily access to MTV's vast audience. People from my neighborhood weren't watching MTV. Not only were they not watching MTV, but it wasn't even available to be watched. Back in the day, either the cable provider didn't offer the station, or it was buried in a premium package that subscribers had to pay extra for. Now, if you were struggling to make ends meet because you were barely making minimum wage, you sure as hell weren't tripping on adding an extra channel to your cable bill. At that time, MTV was a big hit in the suburbs. Even though it was already a household fixture in certain homes, I was still slow to realize just how influential this platform really was.

The reality was that through my little *MTV Jams* program, all these white kids in rural and suburban cities across the country and around the world could be introduced to Black artists. They could learn a little bit about Black culture and creativity. Some of these kids who watched the show had no interactions whatsoever with people who looked like me. They didn't see Black people in their own communities, schools, or social circles. They were insulated and clueless. I mean really clueless, not like the movie *Clueless*. The language of music was bringing me in front of different types of people. It was breaking color and class barriers and shattering geographical stereotypes. I started to realize my unique opportunity to really elevate different kinds of artists and perspectives to the masses.

Before influencer culture happened on the 'Gram, you had me on MTV.

I was a social chameleon with cool Fresh Prince vibes. My relaxed fun-loving style of interviewing would make artists feel disarmingly comfortable about opening their souls about their lives and passions. I made them feel at home in my space, creating an environment of understanding and protection of their simple truths—of their authentic journey. There were no airs of pretentiousness or corporate jargon with me. I worked for a corporation, but I ran my shit like a cool conversation in your car or an animated debate in your local barbershop. This was home. I would leave my audiences busting at the seams feeling like they had just been to a comedy show and concert all at the same time; all of this without leaving MTV's head-quarters.

I had what they could never deliver through any of their other VJs. Don't get it twisted, there was absolutely nothing shabby about being an MTV VJ. Actually, those that became VJs were virtual nobodies who were catapulted into fame's spotlight usually with very little formal training or experience. They usually just had the "it" factor that execs liked. It was a great gig and provided a certain type of exposure and celeb-rity that was cool. I was just a little bit more. I represented the authenticity of the times and from the streets. I was the voice, eyes, and ears from the other side of the tracks. I was the beat-ing pulse of hip-hop up in those halls. The suits were good at pushing buttons, analyzing data, and calculating profits. I was good at reading the tempo of the streets, polishing it up a bit, then turning it into bankable content for the world to fall in love with the flava!

Being a master multitasker, I was on MTV and still doing

stand-up gigs every chance I got. The music business was on fire, especially in the R&B and rap sectors. Hip-hop was finally getting its appropriate due. Everything was going well. Another type of underground music kicking off in the northern West Coast area was Grunge music, and it was taking the white community by storm. It was their version of what hip-hop was to young Black kids. It harnessed the angst and struggles of growing up without the bubble gum varnish. It spoke to the darker side of youth. Alternative music was also simmering. Rock bands were killing and appealing to younger audiences. There was so much innovative talent being highlighted, records were selling and flying off the shelves. It was a bomb time to be in the business. Money was flowing everywhere. And, it was a great time to be a funny-ass comedian too.

As savvy as I was, and with all this big shit going on, it was hard to believe I still didn't fully internalize just how big MTV was in the cultural sense. I was on MTV every day; actually, four or five times a day. Despite this takeover on the airwaves, I never saw myself on TV.

Remember, I still didn't have MTV at my house. I would hear friends make passing comments here and there about stuff I was doing and interviews I had done. One of my boys actually had access to MTV at his crib and that's how I would periodically catch snippets of my show. HBO was also new and buzzing at the time. Just based on the types of icons and people I was meeting, I felt like somebody had given me a VIP pass to this amazing world of entertainment and I was flying by the seat of my pants. I didn't have a lot of experience with famous people, and ironically, I didn't even realize I had become one of them!

The first incident that made it crystal clear to me that I had reached a certain level of fame occurred when I went to Minneapolis, Minnesota, for work. MTV was filming in the Mall of America, the biggest damn mall in the world. I'd never seen a mall with an amusement park in it. Never, ever! I even think that bitch had a zoo or something crazy like that as well. I was out there filming a show with my fellow VJs Daisy Fuentes and Kennedy (Lisa Kennedy Montgomery). The executives at MTV often liked to bring together popular VJs from different programs, to do joint programming, therefore cross-pollinating audiences. It was actually brilliant marketing that worked spectacularly. During a break from filming, I made my way to the Footlocker store because I'd always been a Sneaker Head. I just never had the money to fuel my secret passion until that point.

As I was focused on picking up the latest kicks and checking out what I wanted to purchase, suddenly, out of nowhere, I see little white kids coming from everywhere and staring at me. I said to myself, I see white people! These kids were peeking inside, looking through the window, whispering to each other, and pointing right at me. What the hell is going on? As they were pointing in my direction and smiling, I kept looking behind me to see what they were pointing at. It hadn't even dawned on me that the fish in the fishbowl was me! The next thing I knew, there were twenty white kids assembling in front of me. Then forty white kids. The number turned into sixty, then about one hundred white kids all crammed into this little-ass store. I lost count. They kept coming and piling in, crowding around me. Seeing the massive crowd, the manager came over to me and said, "Excuse me, sir. Are you famous?"

Baffled by the question I said, "No. I have never been to Minnesota in my life. I have no idea how anybody in Minneapolis would know me if I've never been here before."

That's when one of the white kids looks at me and asks, "What is your name? Are you Bill Bellamy?"

I look at him confused and slowly said, "Yes. How do you know me?"

He grinned uncontrollably almost busting at the seams. "You're on MTV!" he said proudly. He then turns and screams out to the other kids in the back of the crowd, "That is him! It's really Bill Bellamy!" With that realization, all the kids started yelling, screaming, and damn near crying. All those excited and happy white kids start pressing in a little closer to greet me, say what's up, or get a quick hug. I realized two things at that moment. First, what the fuck, I was famous! The second thing I realized was that I needed security to go to Footlocker.

After that incident, I called my mom, saying, "Mom, I think I'm FAMOUS!"

She laughed and said, "You are to me, baby!" Then she continued, "The hard work is finally paying off for you." It was truly a cool defining moment I will remember forever.

Some of the best moments of my life will always be linked to the endless list of amazing emerging talents I got to interview. My style for my interviews was just simply being a fan myself. I always thought of the questions that the fans would want to know. I did my interviews from the perspective of how a fan of that particular artist would do it. Instead of me being Bill Bellamy the interviewer, in every opportunity I was Bill Bellamy the fan of the artist. It was an endearing approach that made the artist feel flattered and comfortable. It was intentional, but not calculated. I was so enthusiastic and inquisitive that it worked. My goal was to ask artists the intimate, detailed questions that only a real fan of that artist would ask. As the cherry on top, I would do it with a smile, wink, and laugh. Sometimes my friendly nature worked a little too well for me.

I remember when I was interviewing Mariah Carey. Her husband and manager at the time, music executive Tommy Mottola, made certain that she was always traveling with all these Sopranos-looking dudes. They were four big-ass, greasy hair, trench-coat wearing security guys that were with her at all times . . . I mean old-school mob-looking and intimidating as fuck. During the interview, Mariah and I were laughing and having a good time and they abruptly called a timeout. They were like, "Stop! Stop! Cut!" They turned to me and said in a really slow and deliberate tone, "Hey kid. Just talk about the album." I got their message loud and clear. They thought I was flirting with her ass and they nixed all that coy laughter shit right quick. Hey, I'm no dummy and definitely no punk, but they didn't need to say another damn word.

When you clicked with an artist you genuinely clicked. When I'd snag Janet Jackson for interviews, I wanted to know how it is that she could be so shy and soft-spoken in person, but be so sexually confident and provocative in her music? Where was the segue to that person? Because when I would hang out with her, I could barely hear her damn voice. Her voice was so sweet and soft; she is sort of shy and timid. In person she comes off like a baby fawn you instantly want to cuddle and protect. And then, when you close your eyes and listen to her music, I picture this ravenous, sexually confident, warrior-like female that could fuck shit up! I mean it sounds like she could really tear down the damn house! So, was it an alter ego, or was this the person that she always wanted to be and just becomes her when she's singing her music? Real talk, it was like some split personality shit! The total switch-up fascinated me for real.

One memorable Janet interview had me looking like a pubescent schoolboy. It was 1993 and I was talking about Janet Jackson every day on MTV like she was my homegirl. I was doing all kinds of funny stuff to introduce her videos, talking about how fine she was and her super-talented family. I just really enjoyed the work she was putting out. At that time, her music video that was on fire was *That's the Way Love Goes*. It was a fun-loving upbeat song that expressed the feeling of love and all the crazy things it does to you. I talked about it literally every damn day. Little did I know, I would eventually meet the girl in the video.

I don't know if I would say I had a crush on Janet Jackson . . . but I did! Who didn't have a crush on her back then? It was like a crush in a cool kind of innocent way. My crush started when I watched this girl on *Good Times* growing up. One of the only Black shows on television. Her brother was Michael Jackson, and she came from a very famous Black family. She comes from Black royalty and was the princess of the empire. There were so many reasons to love Janet.

I was in Los Angeles to do the interview and Janet was in her dressing room. Before the interview started, I was standing there talking to all of the dancers and camera crew, making small talk, joking around, and just shooting the shit. Janet came out of the room and I tried to do this awkward kind of a formal handshake thing with her. Before I knew what was happening, she leaned in and gave me a warm embrace. Just like she had known me forever! I felt straight-up cornball silly!

She said, "Bill, I'm so glad you could make it."

The woman was gorgeous, kind, and had the most amazing smile. I was completely captivated and lost for words, to say the least. At that time I was supposed to be "the man," but I was far from it in that moment. I was the mush! I was more like boo boo the fool!

When we started filming the show, Janet delicately put her hand on my chest. Oh my God—this girl was blowing my mind! Then her cheek followed and she snuggled in. I almost blacked out on live TV. She smelled so damn good. To witness the embarrasing meltdown yourself, go to YouTube to see the receipts. Pay special attention to how my face looked during that moment, I was not playacting. I was really having a moment on live television. Here I was with this gorgeous sexy woman who's a bona fide superstar. I finally got to meet my childhood crush and here she was laying her head on my chest! I said to myself, If they don't hurry up and go to commercial break, I'm not going to be able to continue my freaking job. Please do not let me embarrass myself in front of all these camera people. Please, Lord, please. It was hilariously written all over my face. The dancers were right there getting a good laugh at the incredible melting host.

After my Janet interview, there was this interesting vibe between us. I would learn later on that the vibe was completely mutual. We hung out for a while and I could tell my sense of humor really resonated and allowed her to let her guard down. I had a way of connecting to people who could be more closed off; it was one of my secret powers. Everyone thought we had something going on, but we were just good friends. Her next album, *The Velvet Rope,* came out in 1997. Janet was doing all kinds of promotions for it and she was coming back to MTV to promote it. Prior to her visit, she hit me up and said, "Yo, B, what's up? I miss you. Haven't seen you in a long time." I loved this chick. She was super cool and had really friendly energy about her. In many ways, she reminded me of myself, very easygoing. On the day of her actual interview, I finished up all my interviews for that day at MTV. Janet came to the studio with the whole damn label in tow. I mean, she looked like she had about a million people in her entourage. The publicist, assistants, assistants to assistants—Boss shit! She was definitely in control.

This reminds me of one day when I was at home on the phone talking to this woman I was dating at the time. Suddenly, my other line beeps indicating that there was another call coming through. I click over to answer and hear,

"Hey, B."

"Hey, who's this?" I answer.

"Janet!"

"Janet who?" This was my home number—my private line. I never gave anybody that number, especially when it came to business.

"Um, Janet . . ."

I gave a laugh, then click. I hung up the line and went back to chatting it up with my girl on the other line. I didn't have time for no prank calls and I just knew that was a gag. I said to my girl, "Yo, man, people be bullshitting, you know? Playing games on the phone and childish shit." I continue talking for a bit, I was in my zone, and I hear my other line beep again. I hesitantly click back over and sure enough, it was the same voice as before, saying, "Hello, did you hang up on me?"

"What?" I say this time with a little annoyance in my voice. I still didn't believe that Janet Jackson was calling my house phone.

"Did you just hang up on me?"

"I don't have time to play games. Who is this for real?"

"It's Janet Jackson."

"You bullshitting?" I ask. "Are you serious?" I knew it was the same voice and instantly broke out in a cold sweat.

"Yeah, and you hung up on me!" she said, giving me a little bit of her alter ego sass.

"One minute," I say, hurriedly clicking back over and saying, "Bye, girl! I got Janet Jackson on my other line!" Click!

When I switched back over to Janet, she continued, "Man, B, I got a favor to ask of you. I want to see what you think. I got a great idea."

"What's up?" I respond quickly, ready to jump into action. Why wouldn't I? This was "the Janet" calling to get a favor from me!

"I'm on my Velvet Rope Tour right now and my opening act is leaving to do another gig. I want to use a comedian. What do you think about coming out on a road with me? It would be fun, right? We could do twenty cities, or whatever. I'll send you my dates. Let me know what you think. I'll talk to your people and set it up and you can come out."

My first thought was, Yes Ma'am! Now, you got to understand, I did the Def Comedy Jam Tour, and we were doing twenty-five hundred to five thousand seaters. Now, I was going to be on stage with this woman with twenty thousand plus seats a night? That was a humongous jump!

"Hell, yeah!" I said enthusiastically. I didn't know what it would be like, but I knew I was in. This was the pinnacle within the entertainment game—to be worthy enough to pull in people in an arena. I had worked my way up to arena status! This only happened when you were at the top of your game and your fans would drive ticket sales through the roof. I knew they weren't piling into the arena just to see my ass, but I would benefit from Janet's superstar power. I had never been around anyone who was at that stage in their career. This shit was officially cool as fuck! I couldn't believe she thought to include me! It was an honor.

Janet's tour manager called and gave me my plane tickets. FYI, I had never had this level of white-glove service before for work, not on this level. I mean, with Def Comedy Jam Tour, we did tour buses, but this was like the real deal; like rock star–level operations. My itinerary arrived like clockwork. I got my Velvet Rope Book and my special VIP-access laminated pass as well. It was official.

Night after night I was out there on stage in big-ass stadiums doing jokes for twenty, sometimes thirty minutes before introducing Janet Jackson to Boston, to Philly, to Chicago. At the time I was still a young, new comedian coming up in the game. Now I was doing it opening for the hottest artist in the world. Damn, I had just gotten my feet wet at MTV! It still gives me chills to remember the loud booming announcement that would say, "Now for our special guest comedian, Bill Bellamy from MTV." All the people would go bananas! It was surreal.

This was a monumentally unexpected opportunity and blessing for me. I got to see first-hand what it was like to be Janet Jackson. To actually see what it took to dominate at the highest level. This was the level I wanted to get to. I mean, this is the type of stardom I worked so hard to get to, right? The feeling of twenty-five thousand people screaming, cheering, and singing your songs at the top of their lungs. I remember being on that stage and seeing myself on the jumbotron on both sides of the stadium. Two flipping jumbotrons meant there were so many people at that event that they had to put you on the massive screen. Big shit! The fans wanted to see you up close from every angle. That's crazy. The show had a major funding and mega-production value. Having that many people love you at the same time and directly receiving all that love was overwhelming. The whole experience was epic, but was it real? I had a strange feeling that experience could have become an unhealthy addiction.

Touring with Janet really showed me what was possible. By this point, I had learned to believe in myself and operate in the business of Bill Bellamy. More than believing in myself, I now experienced the pinnacle of possibility for myself. If you're rollin' with someone like Janet Jackson, selling out arenas, there wasn't any bigger. During the tour, I realized there were different levels to success; especially when it came time to get my check.

Most people have never heard of "the money room." Yes, I said *the money room*. Not a money envelope, not a suitcase . . . a room! The money room held all the box office receipts. A lot of times it consisted of millions of dollars in cold hard cash. This was the first time I'd ever seen stacks of pure money everywhere, just like we were in a gangster movie. Guarding this room were large stone-faced dudes packing major heat. They had their big accented by smaller guns strapped firmly to their sides. Nobody was concealing anything; they wanted you to see why you shouldn't try to fuck with them. That's when you know there is "real" paper in the building.

The first time I went to collect my payment on the tour, I tentatively approached the huge thick metal door and leaned into the peephole. Suddenly it slid open with a loud BANG! Just like a loud-ass prison door slamming shut. Some crazy-looking private security dude opened the door and barked, "Do you want to get paid in cash or check?" The energy got really tense and there were no smiles, jokes, or anything to be found anywhere. Those dudes were securing that bread and there was absolutely nothing to laugh about. They gave me a little head nod and ushered me inside with a brief, "What up, bro?" and kept it moving. There was so much neatly stacked money in every corner it was mesmerizing. Completely aware it wasn't mine, I still held the hope that maybe one day it could be. Instantly aware that my ass was getting just a tiny part of that room, I still floated in on cloud nine. Trust me, I had zero complaints!

I got my "little money" and said to my boy, who was waiting outside for me, "Yo, man, we got to get to that level. That's the money room. That's the level where you blow up! That's the Eddie Murphy. That's the Madonna, Rolling Stone's, Bruce Springsteen room. In that room, they pay you because of your talent and your power." I love that about this game, and it still pushes me to this day. I always tell people when you're shooting for the stars, surround yourself with other stars, because before you know it, you will look around and be in the galaxy.

Janet is a dope chick because she didn't have to treat me like I was family. She even threw me a surprise birthday party on tour. She really took care of me and never treated me like just a disposable opening act, like some big-named artists are known to do. As big as she was, Janet recognized I was up and coming up and showed value and respect for what I was bringing to the table. She showed great humanity and humility in providing me a space to shine. I will always give her major props for that and show her mad love just like she showed me!

Back on earth at MTV headquarters, I even got to ask goofy, but fucking genius, questions to music legends like Prince. I remember when I quizzed him about his unique choice in clothing. I asked, What would make you wear boots? Of all the shoes . . . and you chose boots? I also wanted him to answer, What would make you have your booty cheeks out and wear a blouse of all things? And, on top of it, you always pull the hottest chicks! What's up with that? How'd you do it, Roger? Tell me. Inappropriate questions if you were interviewing Prince for *20/20*, but perfect when you were at MTV *Jams*.

I reminisce about the time I was preparing to interview the King of Pop himself, Michael Jackson. There are no introductions needed. Michael Jackson was and is so legendary that I just couldn't contain myself. At that time, he was working with big-time producers like Teddy Riley, Rodney Jerkins (aka Darkchild), R. Kelly, and Timberland, who were all submitting their top music to Michael to use for his albums. Everybody knew Michael Jackson had an unlimited budget with the label so they were all trying to hit one out of the ballpark for him. I didn't even know where to begin actually. Even though I knew the work this musical genius had created backward and forward, there were still so many things I was curious about. I wanted to ask Michael Jackson so many things, but when it got to the editing and production phase, a whole bunch of my questions were shot down. Sony looked at them and said, "Nope, nope, nope, nope, and double nope!"

They cut my fifty questions down to eight or ten. I stayed up all night before the interview banging them out; die-hard fan-type shit. I wanted to know, What was your dad like when you were coming up? What was Gary, Indiana, like for you guys? How did you know it was time to break away from your family group and go solo? What was that like? What did it feel like to be ten years old, the leader of a family band, and have all your grown brothers want to be you? What kind of responsibility is it to know that you're carrying your whole family, and you're a child? See, I would have wanted to ask that question because that's how brilliant Michael Jackson was. It was crazy if you really stopped to think about the group's dynamics and the incredible level of success they attained. You mean to tell me that a twelve-year-old baby boy was better than all those grown-ass niggas in the band? Good enough where he got to be the lead? Sorry, I love you to death Jermaine, but you just ain't it! How did that conversation go? Awkward!

Let me backtrack a bit, and share how the infamous Michael Jackson Times Square interview all came about. I was surreptitiously picked, by Michael himself, to host the world premiere of his *You Are Not Alone* video in 1995, which featured his then-wife Lisa Marie Presley. It was during the hyper-Michael fandom phase when Michael and Janet had teamed up to do their highly anticipated co-branded video, for their single "Scream" on Michael's 1995 *HIStory: Past, Present, and Future, Book I* album. It was an edgy, groundbreaking, space-aged music video that got them both a ton of accolades. It was also the most expensive video ever made to date. I mean, everybody was talking about it before it even came out. When it premiered, all the hype was well-deserved because that shit was so lit! Imagine this, it was the night of the MTV Video Music Awards and I was presenting the award for Video of the Year, with hip-hop legend Notorious B.I.G. Being on stage with Biggie was crazy enough; my night could have ended there and it would have been amazing. We opened the envelope and the winner for Video of the Year was the song "Scream" by Michael Jackson and Janet Jackson. Wow, Michael, Janet, Biggie, and I were all on stage at the same damn time! When we all eventually made our way backstage, Michael and I were making small talk and then he said to me, "I love what you do with my sister. You know, you're really good and you have such good energy in your interviews. I want you to be a part of my music."

I was like, what the fuck did I just hear this King of Pop say to me? Whaaaaaaat? I said, "Yeah, Michael, whatever. I love you, bro. Whatever you want. Let's do it." The next thing I knew, I was requested to be the person to debut Mike's huge "You Are Not Alone" song, which was also on his *HIStory* album.

Once I got my marching orders, the pressure was really on! This was no amateur assignment. This was going to be the first time a music video debuted on all the major networks simultaneously. I mean it was going to be on MTV and every other competitive network all at the same time, and I was the one hand-picked to usher it in! Shhhhiiiiiit, this was damn near like a baptism by the king himself. I had to make sure I looked good, sounded good, and smelled good too. This is my childhood hero. I knew every single Michael Jackson and Jackson 5 song like the back of my hand. I had a dream about this moment. When I actually got the call confirming the interview, I headed straight to Barneys New York with MTV's credit card in hand. I'll never forget the Park Avenue Barneys men's store; it was crazy luxurious. I think I must have dropped fifteen grand up in that place. I was buying designer suits, ties, shirts, and shoes. Dope stuff! When MTV got wind of the money I had racked up on the corporate card, they said, "Take that shit back immediately! Are you crazy? We're not spending that kind of money for you to do an interview, Bill!" Then came the hammer. They said, "Pick one outfit, and it better not be over two thousand dollars!"

Thinking back, it was such an outrageous stunt, but at the time I tried to push back defiantly, "What? Y'all ain't got no money? Ain't this a network? You know that's Michael Jackson, right?" Eventually, I backed down and returned everything except for this one really fly tan Giorgio Armani suit.

Even though I was so damn proud of that interview and honored to be chosen, deep down I wasn't in love with how it turned out. The finished product didn't reflect the typical style or flavor that I was known for. Did I sell out? In short—no. I just had no choice but to comply with the powers that be. The Machine that ruled much of the industry was Sony Music Inc. I didn't get to ask Michael the questions I really wanted to because the interview got "corporatized" and "prescrubbed." The result was just vanilla to me; no BB flavor. I was a bit disappointed, to be honest. I felt like his real fans would have wanted to know the list of questions I originally prepared because I've wanted to know those things my whole life. The types of questions I had created were the type of conversational questions that got you the info you weren't getting elsewhere. I went after the behind-the-scenes, under the veil, kitchen table conversation type of shit that nobody else was delivering.

My brand plan was manifesting itself. My Janet tour, the amazing rapport established with other artists, a growing body of diverse work, and groundbreaking interviews, I wanted my career to ignite and explode as I had seen others' careers do. I was starting to wonder if there was more for me than just MTV. That's the thing about exposure. Once you're exposed, it's impossible to put that genie back in the bottle.

5

RAP LEGENDS

"LEGENDS"

Song by Juice WRLD

When friends become like family, they can transform your life for eternity. The close trusting bond I developed with Tupac will stay with me forever. Pac and I did a bunch of stuff together both on and off camera. He used to come to my shows all the time in New York and we would bump into each other everywhere because we knew all the same people. He used to say to me, "You is a funny motherfucker, B! Goddamn, B." He was also really tight with rapper Treach, from the New Jersey–based group Naughty By Nature. So, whenever he was going to be in the studio with those cats he would come to my shows in Jersey too.

On one particular occasion, my sister, Karen, and I were standing outside after one of my shows when Pac rolled up in a blacked-out car. I decided to introduce him to her because she'd always been a huge fan. She never knew that I knew Tupac and hung with him regularly. When I saw the car, I said to her, "I may introduce you to somebody, but don't act crazy. Just, just be normal. Just act normal!"

She said, "Who is it?"

I answered, "It's Tupac Shakur."

Her eyes bugged out for a brief second, then she got a really cynical look on her face and said, "Billy, you do not know Tupac."

"Yes, I do, and I'm gonna bring him over here." By this time she was sitting in my car. "I want you to act normal," I added again.

She rolled her eyes and said to me sarcastically, "I'm not going to trip, Bill. God, I've met famous people before."

At that moment, Tupac knocked on the passenger side car window and my sister was literally face-to-face with him. Staring her right in the face with that magnetic Pac grin he said, "Hey how are you doing?"

I had never seen anything like it, and I had seen my share of screaming fans having a meltdown; my sister done lost her mind. She started to scream "Ahhhhhhhhh!" right in the man's damn face. After her "moment," she finally blurted out, "You are so beautiful. I love you so much. You are sooooo handsome."

I was sitting there mortified, horrified, and all the other "-fieds" you could think of. After some small talk between us, he went back to his car and pulled off. I turned to my sister and said to her, "Girl! Didn't I tell your ass to be cool? To just act normal . . . Damn!"

She said, "Bill, you don't understand. He's just so amazing. He's so handsome. He's Pac . . . I just love him!"

I added chuckling, "You know he's got a bulletproof vest on so chill with the stalker shit!"

That was just one of those really dope moments that came with my level of fame and access. I could share it with the ones I loved. My sister said she would never forget the time her big brother introduced her to Tupac Shakur. To this day she treasures that memory dearly and so do I. Thanks for the memories, Pac!

What was really cool about Tupac, and what people didn't understand before all that stuff went left, was that me, Biggie, and him were really, really tight. We all had mutually overlapping friends that brought us together. We went to the same parties and local joints like Nell's nightclub in New York. We always seemed to be in the same place at the same time so we ended up spending a lot of time hanging out together. I remember they introduced me to how you roll a proper blunt when we were in Atlanta shooting the Da Brat music video for "I'll Give It 2 You." We were all sitting in the trailer and they were smoking weed together, like the best of friends. It was the first time I'd ever seen dudes rolling blunts mixed with tobacco; it was like they were professional motherfuckers. Shit, to be honest, before that encounter I didn't even know what the term "blunt" meant. You should have seen me. I was like a nosy-ass little kid sitting at the edge of my seat asking lots of cornball questions: What this? Why y'all taking all the tobacco out? What you gonna do with that? Damn, you could tell my ass was green as fuck.

They looked at me amazed and said, "Damn, dog! You don't smoke blunts?" I was up in that trailer high as hell with these two goofballs and I hadn't even smoked anything. We had fun together even though I clearly wasn't as "of the streets" as they were. They saw in me another way to be, and I appreciated that. Even though they had made it to the big time, they were still real-ass dudes.

When Tupac got locked up at Rikers Island, I got a letter from him, which I probably still have in a box in my mom's basement. In essence, it said, "Yo, B man, I need a favor. I'm asking all my people to do me a favor and I want you to be in my video *Temptations*." He went on to say, "When I get out of here. I am going to do my first interview with you, bro!"

I thought, Oh snap! Sure enough, when Pac got out of jail everybody wanted to interview him. Every news station, every magazine, newspaper—everybody! When it finally got out that I was doing the interview, everybody was hot as hell! I mean fucking scorched! It wasn't just an interview; it was history, and everybody knew it. For me, I wanted to do right by a friend and take care of him. I knew at that moment it was some Barbara Walters level shit and I gotta do him right because of our friendship. Tupac was a real fucking cat and loyal to the core. To show you how unaffected he was, Tupac got out of jail one time and rolled up to a black-tie Clive Davis party at the Beverly Hills Hotel wearing a Red Wings hockey jersey and bandana smoking a cigarette. Mind you, it was a nonsmoking event. You had Madonna, Whitney Houston, and all other types of big-time celebrities losing their shit when he walked in there. Nobody had expected him. He didn't even blink a fucking eye or think twice about it.

Pac felt at home everywhere and exuded a raw, natural confidence and swagger I had never experienced before. He was doing mythical shit that I had never heard of a Black man doing. He was a legend in his own time. He got shot, but he lived. He had a shootout with the cops in Atlanta and beat the case. How many times do you see people keep getting shot and winning?

It was crazy! That's why everybody thought he'd survive that ambush in Las Vegas because he kept winning in the past. His death still bothers me tremendously even today. I took the news very, very hard. Tupac Shakur was my brother and one of the most talented guys I have ever come across.

Six months later when Biggie got killed, I was on a plane flying into Los Angeles. I looked at my pager that was buzzing with a message scrolling across the screen that read: "Rapper Biggie Smalls shot." I was about to land and I said to myself, Oh my God. Not again! Not again! When I landed and was making my way through the terminal, I remember seeing rapper De Brat on the news on the ground crying outside the venue and somebody was trying to hold her up. I thought, "Oh no, did Brat get shot too?" I didn't know what the hell to think anymore. I was in such a daze. Then I heard that he had died. When I'd learned all the details about his death, I remember when Biggie told me he was coming out to California. I distinctly remember thinking, Why is Big coming to California right now? It don't make no sense! Why are they doing that shit now? It was too rough right now for Big to go out there. There was such East Coast/West Coast beef and the situation was too hot. They needed to wait for it to cool down a bit. They came anyway despite all the warnings. To make matters even worse, Biggie had that song "Going Back to Cali" out. The lyrics said: "I'm going, going back back to Cali Cali!" It appeared to be taunting and disrespectful—flying in the face of the very real territorial coast-versus-coast drama that we were in the grips of. I managed to stay above the fray of it all because I was in a safe zone of sorts. Everybody knew I was doing it for the music. There was no separation for me between East or West Coast swag; it was all just good damn music. I gave them both shine and love. It was still a scary time. Niggas were getting killed left, right, and center. Ones with money and fame. Niggas who you thought had made it. I had a love for both those dudes, and the crazy thing is they had a love for each other too.

It wasn't all bulletproof vest interactions. There were those cats that were as cool as cool could be and just needed a little more weed to get by. My dog Snoop Dogg—I'll never forget the time my crew and I went to his house to interview him. It was bonkers; he held everybody hostage. Snoop said he ain't doing the interview until he got a shoebox of weed. Yes, you heard me, a shoebox full of weed! It went a little something like this . . .

The van was loaded with sound crew, producers, lighting and technical dudes, all ready to capture this great interview with Snoop. It had been planned for weeks and it was a big "get" for my show. Snoop was on fire. He was doing some major stuff with DPG, made up of rappers Daz & Kurupt and Tha Dogg Pound Gangsta's. We get to the house and Snoop answers the door and says, "Yo. What's up, nephew? I have a request, nephew. Now, I can't do this interview today."

I look at him blinking, my crew all behind me ready to work and shit. I say, "What? I just flew all the way out here from New York, dog! Why? What's up?"

Straight faced he says to me, "Eh, man, I need me a shoebox of some motherfucking weed!"

I said, "Right now?"

"Eh, until you can make that motherfucker happen, you, Bill Bellamy, ain't you!"

Stunned, I head back to the producer sitting in the van parked outside his house and say, "Yo, I got some bad news y'all. Shit, Snoop said he ain't doing the interview until we get him a shoebox of weed."

The producer shot back, "Whhhhaaat? Where the fuck do we get a shoebox of weed? How much is in a fucking shoebox of weed?"

That's when the little Mexican dude in production, who was sitting in the back of the van, chimed in. Out of nowhere, he said, "Like three ounces!"

"What?" I asked.

"A shoebox of weed is about three to four ounces."

"Are you serious? I don't know anything about no weed shit, so whatever," I said. "Where are we going to get that?" I was completely baffled and deflated.

He was like, "I know where we can get weed like that. I'll call my cousin." So, he calls his cousin and we begin to gather up all our petty cash we had on hand. Once he had all the money, the production guy takes off in a little car and was gone for about forty minutes. When he came back the whole motherfucking shoebox was full of some petty cash weed!

I went up to Snoop's door again and presented him with the box full of weed. This fool says, "Well, enter nephew. Now let's get this motherfucking interview started! This motherfucker went and got this shit, homie. Let's blaze this shit up!" He had me cracking up and I gained his respect that day, I'm sure!

My authenticity and real connection to the street's cultural icons set me apart and gave me that special something that MTV needed in order to connect with Black and Brown audiences. Russell Simmons knew it too and that's why he signed me a few years prior when he saw me at the filming of Uptown Comedy Club in Harlem. He said, "I'm starting a management company and I want to be a part of your future. A part of your success. I want to be there for you because I think you are outstanding. You're it. You're it. Bitches love you and I love that. That's it! Also, you're presentable and you've got that perfect combination of talent, intelligence, and street humor on the right platform. Fucking brilliant! It's going to get you into movies and whatever else you want to do. If I can't make at least a million dollars off of you, then I wouldn't manage you. I see you making a lot of money. Real talk." Even after such a full-throated pitch to manage me, every time I'd call Russell Simmons, the conversation would go like this: "Hey, Russell, what's up? How are you doing?"

"Who? Who is this? Who is calling?" he'd ask, as serious as a motherfucker.

"It's Bill. Bill Bellamy. You manage me, remember?"

"Oh yeah. Oh yeah, what's up? I remember. I knew your voice. I know you." I crack up every time I think about Russell.

As scattered and funny as Russell could be, when it came to making deals in business, he was a fucking great white shark! When I was a few years into the MTV gig and making waves, Russell would say, "Yo, B, you're the nigga up in there at MTV. You're like Puff, but not Puff. You in. You're articulate enough to make the white people comfortable. You gotta push it. You got to get our music out there. You got to get us all the way there, B! That's your purpose. It's cultural, it's purposeful." I already felt the same way, but I took his perceptive advice to heart. Russell was the one that made MTV give me more money at the time. Russell lobbied for me saying, "Bill's number one. He's the number one VJ on your channel and your network. I don't care who else is on there, he's got to be the highest-paid!" At that time MTV was notorious for not paying people very well at all until Russell came into the picture. He looked out for me and secured an unprecedented deal against all odds. That's Russell with the muscle right there.

Music is a universal language. You can almost feel it before you hear it. It can bring people together, build bridges where none existed, and it has the innate ability to linger and allow listeners to digest otherwise controversial messages. Music was also the conduit to my education about new horizons, people, and cultures. I learned so much from these artists. They gave me an opportunity to understand their world and so did the fans. To gain knowledge about the hopes and dreams of a culture where color lines and territory didn't matter. Where there was just harmony and good damn music. The simple truth is that MTV needed a face that could make white America comfortable. A personality that was magnetic. I had a mix of humor, just a bit of nerdiness, and an eye for talent that led me seamlessly from interviews with the biggest artists of the day to the offices of MTV execs. I was able to slowly and methodically earn the trust of the head honchos by opening doors that had been closed previously to many talented, upcoming Black R&B and hip-hop stars. The fans resoundingly responded to having more access to Black music being featured on the network. It was the right time and I was the right person. I wielded my sword, and a newfound celebrity within the C-Suite, to give my people a shot at the brass ring. For this, I remain immensely proud.

6

PAYING IT FORWARD
AND BACKWARD

———

"MONEY, POWER
& RESPECT"

Song by the Lox (featuring DMX and Lil' Kim)

I was able to become a success because there was nothing that I could not do. I'm an observer by nature. Growing up, I loved to grab chunks of knowledge from watching how different cats moved about my block intermingling with folks. They taught me something. In adult life, I would observe how my peers, mentors, and idols navigated deals and put together opportunities. I would look beyond the obvious and always question what motivated people to move the way they did. Plenty of times I'd see my idols do something and I'd say to myself, I know how to do that as well! Yep, I would have played it the same damn way, or nah, I'd never have done it like that. I would have done it way different so it could have made more of an impact. My brain never shuts off. Coming up in the streets teaches you how to always be ready to diversify your approach at the drop of a hat. How to turn sour-ass lemons into the sweetest damn lemonade. Hey, if our washing machine was broken, we'd flip it and wash our clothes in the tub, without even missing a beat. I was conditioned to be creative, resourceful, and endlessly resilient.

If I was a rapper, I would be Jay-Z. Yeah, he's the rapper that I think personifies the way I feel about my life, how I talk and carry myself; he would be the closest example to it. Jay knows the hustle of the streets, but he can clean that hustle up and take it into the boardroom, to the studio, and to the movie screen. Jay accomplishes all this while laughing his way to the bank as cool as a motherfucking cucumber. That's the type of path I was on. Before I could even properly grasp each opportunity, my flexibility had me rubbing elbows with all the right people. Giving me access to sit at the table to influence our culture in a way that might not have happened if I didn't know the blessing and curse behind that style of hustle. If I didn't know when to mute it and when to turn it up. Any successful Black man or woman understands the duality of the role we must play to truly succeed in America. The key is to never stray too far from your truth, or you run the risk of losing yourself. And, no amount of success is worth that.

Sidney Poitier did it back in the day. He opened doors for cats like me to take the baton and run with it. Paying it forward, I came right back around and opened doors for other cats that looked like me and came from similar circumstances. At the end of the day, I aim to make a statement that is authentic and inspirational to Black folks. I had a ton of white fans that

I resonated with as well and it was cool. From the bottom of my heart I appreciated all the love, no disrespect meant, and I never took it for granted. But, the simple truth that I lived with every day was my awareness that representation mattered.

My Blackness made me different. White kids didn't have to worry about whether they were going to see people that looked like them on TV doing big stuff. They saw it everywhere they looked with no effort required. The world was built for white folks. All programming, even the Black shows, were tailored around the perception of white culture. White youth could flip on the movie *Wall Street* and see people that looked just like them, their fathers and uncles making lots of money, conquering the world. White people had lots of visible mentors they could aspire to be like in every sector of life. I was creating my shit for those that didn't. In my comedic world, I welcomed white folks' patronage; I benefited tremendously from their love. I was proud that everyone who stepped into my shows felt comfortable, but I wasn't creating my content with them in mind. For me, it wasn't about not wanting to be inclusive, it was about consciously taking responsibility for my content. As long as I was controlling a live mic, I wanted to make sure that my people were seen and celebrated on the highest level.

That authenticity is the reason why I pushed back so hard during MTV planning meetings. I was the one in the streets. Right there in the recording and producing sessions shoulder to shoulder with the artists. I got scoops because I was on the ground floor when many of these albums were being made. Right there! The only corporate static I got was when I tried to get certain artists, who weren't on corporate's radar, on the show to give them exposure. This portion of my job was a big frigging deal to me. These were the artists that hadn't yet crossed over to "mainstream" recognition. The execs would say, "Well, Bill, you know, we're going by Billboard's numbers . . . yada yada yada." Billboard's analytics were some fucking corny, outdated benchmarks they loved to rely on to predict an artist's success. They measured if songs were tracking at a certain pace to be number one—blah, blah, blah! All that goofy shit! In my opinion, it had very little to do with how people were moving in real time on the streets.

I would plead, "Listen to what I'm saying! I know this song is a hit right now. I don't have to wait until the week-five mark. I'm telling you right now that this song is huge. I can't stress to you enough that this artist is about to blow up! I've seen people dancing to their music. I've seen what happens when it's played in a club. I've seen crowds lose their minds over it. I don't have to wait!" Again, I was on the ground floor every weekend watching it happen. In truth, it was more than just getting the vibe from the clubs. My intel came directly from radio DJs. I was traveling all over the country doing comedy shows and going to the hottest, most banging clubs. After any of my radio interviews, I would ask the DJs what they were playing and what was being requested the most. I was getting the goods on the hot playlist in their town, whether it was Cleveland or San Diego. I was like an undercover A&R exec traveling from Brooklyn to Idaho. DJs would slip me cassettes of local talent who were making noise. I'd listen to them back at my hotel room, and when I found something I connected with, something I knew was dope, I would take it back to the office. That's how I introduced MTV to the artist Ginuwine. The next thing you knew, Ginuwine's music videos were on MTV. I was interviewing artists and starting to travel internationally. Not one of them sitting up there in that boardroom, making decisions, went to clubs; and certainly, no Black clubs. They couldn't possibly know what was really going on. All they could do was track, wait, and try to interpret them dry-ass numbers. Listen, I'm not knocking the numbers. I'm not an idiot. I know it's a numbers game, but numbers don't tell you everything. Numbers are a flattened matrix when you're dealing with something so alive and dimensional like music.

I had done the corporate shuffle thing so I knew that sometimes you've just got to play the game. After my first year, I gained the confidence to speak up and speak my truth so I could really represent our music like it needed to be. I remember one time saying to an executive group, "Why aren't we playing more music by Black artists? Why aren't we debuting more underground acts? This is Music Television; we can't be catering to just one type of crowd. Black kids like to have fun too! I just left Macon, Georgia, and this particular song is the number one jam in the South right now and you're not playing it! How is it that we're not playing a current hit song and we're supposed to be Music Television?" The shit just didn't make sense.

All they could say was, "Oh, whoa, whoa! Ok, Bill. Bill. We get it. We get it."

I recall trying to get MTV to feature a new artist by the name of Usher. Yeah, you've heard of him—that Usher. When I first heard the kid, I knew he was going to be huge! His voice, confidence, and style struck a chord with me and left an impression. MTV execs told me, "No, he seems too young." Who knew if his age would have really been a negative factor. That was their hang up. In my eyes, it was worth a try, because his talent transcended age. I saw the heat and intensity this kid brought with him. You couldn't contain it. He possessed that Michael Jackson magic. What troubled me was that it seemed they'd rather wait until Usher blew up, as opposed to ruffle any feathers by being the ones to launch him to fame. I was disappointed and frustrated! I knew I was right about that kid. And, of course, bam! The next summer Usher was everywhere. He had caught the wave and there was no turning back. That bullet train had left the station and MTV was still thinking about buying a ticket.

It came down to timing and mindset. Being able to spot talent was a gift. It was a game of catching lightning in a bottle and knowing exactly how to handle it. Knowing how to release it for a long and slow burn. I knew how to do that. I was doing it with my own brand, but when you tried maneuvering that risk in the corporate world it was more difficult. In my comedic life, I never asked permission. That was key to being nimble and versatile. I'd press play and just go. In corporate America, you had to get sign-off and buy-in before things could happen. As much as MTV was extremely unconventional, it still had the same clunky structure as traditional corporations. Red tape and executive consensus were often the mood killer and extinguisher to countless promising acts. Not everyone had that eye for talent, and as I previously stated, not everyone was operating off of the same set of facts. Well-intentioned smart people were standing in their own way. If you didn't come from the streets, or even play in them, how the hell could you understand what would set the streets on fire?

The group H-Town from Florida is another example of one of my finds I brought to my little MTV *Jams* lab. After hitting the airwaves with their *Knockin' Da Boots* video during my show, the group skyrocketed into popularity and eventually went platinum. At the time, even though I was in the trenches, I never really got the full impact of what I was doing.

I just thought that I was on a cool scavenger hunt to discover the undiscovered. At first, I didn't even really do it with a plan in mind. I simply enjoyed surrounding myself with people and music that represented what I liked. If I liked it, I knew millions of others might want to see it represented on the channel too. It was a selfish mission that turned into an unselfish drive. MTV became the nexus where cultures met up. It was a place where white kids learned Black lingo and dance moves that they could whip out at parties to make themselves seem cool. It was a transformational time and space because the MTV executives were even caught off guard by how hungry white audiences were for the "otherness" they couldn't authentically bring by themselves. After bringing many undiscovered Black artists to the forefront, I was pretty much granted free rein to fly. I was a Black man showing up as a Black man in all his potential greatness and glory. I was excelling in my zone and helping to usher others into their own.

Years later, when I look at all these artists like Fantasia, Gucci Mane, Jaywop, Future, Migos, Young Jeezy, Salt-N-Pepa, Nelly, Canibus, and Kam that have written songs referencing my Bill Bellamy brand, it fills me with a sense of pride. They reference everything from my hustle, clean-cut appearance, and comedic success, which all means what I've done has stuck! The positivity that these songs portrayed, inserting my name for emphasis, was cool. I had manifested my plan. Bill Bellamy represented winning. It represented success. My whole career I've consciously tried to set a high bar for projects I affiliated myself with. At certain points throughout my career, I'd say to myself, I'm not doing that motherfucking movie, playing that kind of role. That doesn't fit me! Then I'd just walk away. Walk away and leave money sitting on the table for some other actor to swoop in and scoop it up. No shade, but there are some hungry brothers out there that don't have that same quality assurance valve to their work. They're like Mikey from that 1970s Life cereal commercial, "Let's get Mikey . . . Mikey likes it . . . he eats everything!" I've always strived to represent the positive and hopeful side of what being a Black man meant. Educated, charming, strategic, fun-loving, positive, stylish, strong, and successful. My brand had become a piece of our cultural fabric and I took that to heart—that's legacy, that's deep!

Even from early on in my college days, my partner in crime and roommate, Ron Workman, along with our friends Dwyane and Martin, developed a pact with each other. We had already made personal commitments that we were going to do big things in this world. We also vowed to always look like a million bucks—even before we reached that tax bracket. To hold ourselves to those high standards, we decided that we needed to dress the part from early on. Every single day the four of us would get up and put on a suit and tie to go to class. No jeans, no sweats, no Cross Colours hoodies for us. We looked like GQ titans in training, like Wall Street businessmen. Hard bottom shoes and all. Even though we didn't conform to what other kids were doing clothing-wise, we were still very popular freshmen. All popular and all clean-cut. We were extremely outgoing young men who had a shitload of self-confidence to match. The four of us never pledged to any fraternity, but we did develop a well-known persona that had everyone taking notice. We dubbed ourselves the fly guys. I say this to let you know that first impressions have always mattered to me. It's the image that speaks the loudest.

One of the best things about financial success and stability is that you can share it with people in your life. Money can't fix everything, but it usually allows you to worry less about the day-to-day. From the onset, I believed that I was being blessed so I could be a blessing to others, both financially and by increasing access to resources and opportunities. As soon as I could financially swing it, I was taking care of my parents and my younger brother, Julius. I helped to pay for his college tuition and expenses to ensure he got the same opportunities I did. Even though work kept me extremely busy, I promised myself that my baby brother would still feel my presence and influence in his life. I was my brother's keeper and I took that seriously. I'd still make it a priority to pick him up from his sitter in Newark as often as I could and take him to the park for one-on-one time. My relationship with Karen was different because there was only a five-year age gap between us. We pretty much had each other growing up. My baby brother was eighteen years younger than me and damn near like my own kid. By the time he was born I was already off at college starting my own life.

It was important for me to expose my family to as many different places that my new fame allowed me to. To open the window of possibilities to them like they had been opened for me. I brought them to California and took them to a bunch of new and different places. Sometimes successful people don't recognize that even though they're excelling, they still have a responsibility to those who gave them the wind to fly. That's how people get caught up and lose their way.

I also bought my parents' house for them and brought in a fancy interior designer to do a design consultation. After the visit, she laid out a plan to redesign the whole damn house and modernize it. I made sure their space looked slick with nice new top-of-the-line furniture. They were able to splurge on the type of furniture and stuff they wanted but could never dream of affording. My folks were thrilled with the result and it was a perfect thank you for all their sacrifice. Obviously, my mom never had the luxury of an interior decorator before. Not many people in general did, let alone Black people. It was a big, new, and exciting world for them, and I confess that they were a little bit out of their element. Honestly, the Hollywood experience is foreign to almost one hundred percent of the people who get a glimpse, so I understood some of their discomfort. They were simple people with simple tastes. They were also selfless people. Me trying to do all this ostentatious stuff for them was like a grown man putting on a suit that belonged to their four-year-old kid; it just didn't fit. To this day I swear they have never added one new piece of furniture to what the interior designer picked. I mean not one additional thing was added. It's almost like they felt like they were living in a museum. A home filled with precious things they could admire, but never touch.

At first, I was thrilled that my parents liked the outcome of their newly designed home so much that they didn't see the need to change a thing. As the years went on, it began to nag at me. In truth it actually started to annoy me tremendously. I can't quite put my finger on why it did, but it did. I'd say to them sometimes, "You know you can change up the house a bit, right? Add a different pillow, a vase, a chair—anything! Just a bit . . . It's yours. Make it yours!" They'd laugh and wave me off telling me to go away and mind my business.

Eventually, I had to just let it go and let them be. This taught me a very valuable life lesson. It taught me that when you do something for someone, regardless of who it is, that's where your responsibility and opinions should end. I redecorated my parent's home for them, not for me. It made me feel good to help them. This act of kindness, however, didn't give me the right to exert control the situation once it was received. A gift is a gift for a reason. You give it away to make someone else happy; you no longer have possession after that. I had to come to grips with that and let it go. The fact that they didn't get a new little bullshit area rug for x-amount of years was my hang-up, not theirs. My good intentions were well received and that's all I cared about.

In my process of letting the issue go, I had to realize that my family's vision of how to live abundantly was so different than what I had grown to experience as an adult. They had limited exposure to the concept of opulence and excess, so I had to tone down my expectations. Their lens was different. From time to time, I'd take my folks to expensive restaurants in New York City. The ones you'd read about and have to make reservations months in advance if you didn't have the right last name. When we'd go, they would never feel comfortable ordering anything on the menu with a high price tag. As you can imagine at this caliber of restaurant, everything had a large number next to it. They'd be like, "Well, we'll get what you get." Really meekly and shit. When I would tell them to order anything, they'd fight me on it. "No. You know this stuff is too expensive. I don't want you spending this kind of money." I know they meant well, but I wanted to show them the finer side of life and it pissed me off.

I would plead, "But Mom, it's my treat. It's really not a lot of money, I promise you. I can do it!" It always blew my mind in the moment, but I now realize that to them it was just too excessive for their taste. Too fancy, because they always had to operate from a place of necessity throughout their own lives. Nothing extra, because growing up neither they, nor their parents, had anything extra to maneuver with. Yes, they had done far better than their own parents had. They had scaled their own towers of progress not available to generations before them. Even still, it was always a case of just clawing and grinding for the necessities. These highfalutin restaurants were culture shock for them. I was operating on a whole other level of abundances typically only reserved for white people in their days. The shit was really deep when you break it down. I finally realized they weren't rejecting me or my generosity; the concept of "good living" was almost taboo and definitely foreign to them.

My parents were my ground floor and I loved them for that, but if I wasn't careful, their "good enough or just enough" mindset could also hold me back from the full bounty of my blessings. With God's grace, I was able to shoot way past their wildest imagined goals for my future. They didn't have a clue how to digest all the "extra flash" that had now become a part of my type of success. My parents understood the trajectory of going to college, getting a good job, and buying a house. They couldn't grasp the full extent of what I was doing—Hollywood shit! My successes were essentially based on stuff like popularity and exposure, which required a completely different language. They were used to the traditional hallmarks of academic success: lawyer, doctor, or corporate exec. Hell, I couldn't fault them because I was still trying to wrap my head around the shit too, and the shit was happening to me! My rise in entertainment was happening so quickly, and I was just trying to ride the wave. Hanging on for dear life, and that's the truth.

As my friend circle was growing, it was also shrinking simultaneously. I always remember something my uncle said to me once when I was a teenager. The wisdom he shared simplified the idea of friendship for me as I became a grown man. He said, "Sometimes the gifts bestowed upon a man are so grand that those around him can't understand its presence in their life." It seemed deep when he said it to me as a kid, but as I got older, I started to understand just how profound it really was. He was preparing me for what can happen with friendships you thought were solid. With people who you thought had transcended friendship and became your family. My uncle was referring to situations in which you lose connection with some friends because they're not actually vibrating at your level.

His words of wisdom pertained to the concept of energy in motion and how it stays in motion. What happens is that as you elevate in your conscience and life experiences, you unconsciously elevate to new people that are vibrating at your same frequency and pitch. You are automatically drawn to different people who are moving at your same pace. In essence, you change your orbit to propel forward. If you do decide to come down, or reconnect with childhood friends who haven't been on that particular journey of growth, you have to dial it back a bit. You find yourself stepping back to meet them where they are. I experience this when I go back to my old neighborhood after being away for a long time. I have to adapt back into the swing of it all. You can't come back with all that extra razzmatazz shit. It doesn't fit. Your old crew ain't gonna see shit the way you see it because they're vibrating differently. Their orbit of experience and exposure may be more compact. It's physics.

Even me telling my story today is an act of love. I hope you walk away knowing that the ghettos, like where I grew up, are not lost zones of hopeless folks. It's quite the opposite. It's a love-filled community of men, women, and children dreaming bigger dreams than anyone could even imagine. It's a community filled with love, promise, integrity, ingenuity, loyalty, laughter, and some tears. It's overflowing with people beating the odds every fucking day as they fight to be seen. Ghettos are rich with folks who are optimistically making the world run, but sadly not reaping the full rewards of their indelible contributions. They're filled with people who prove daily that the negative stuff we've been taught was intentional and designed to keep us down. Engineered to keep us poor. After all, there's profit in poverty. With poverty comes sickness and a bunch of other profitable ventures. Ask any of those grinning Wall Street clowns. The ghetto is where real stories of bravery come from. Surely, it takes a brave and strong soul to have the audacity to hope when they see very little of it around them. These are my people! This is me, and this is where I came from.

Moving into one's purpose does not mean that you forget where you come from; I have never. It doesn't mean you think of yourself as better or bigger than; I don't. It means you tap into your purpose and fight like hell to bring it into the light. If it makes you fists full of cash then it does. But, even if it only sustains you enough to cover your monthly bills, then it's still worth the struggle because it feeds your soul. If you discover what lights that fire inside of you, consider yourself blessed. Consider yourself even luckier if you can light that fire inside others so they can soar too. That's the work I've done. It's the work I continue to do every damn day of my life. Out loud, and in the quiet hours away from the spotlight. I do it for myself and for others. That's where success lies for me. It lies in the little fires I go around igniting every day. Now, go tell the world Bill Bellamy from the hood told you that!

7

NO BRAKES

"AIN'T NO HALF-STEPPIN'"

Song by Big Daddy Kane

I can't go any further along the path of chronicling my story of becoming the Bill Bellamy you all know today without giving proper credit to one of the most influential figures who helped me see the me in me—Mr. Bob Sumner.

If anyone knows anything about Mr. Sumner, they know that he is a giant! He is savvy, smart, hilarious, intuitive, creative, industrious, authentic, generous—shit, it just doesn't get any better than this man! When you hear Bob Sumner's name mentioned in any damn conversation, it's always linked to some of the biggest, most dynamic men and women who ever stepped up to the mic dreaming to make a living out of making people laugh. The late great Bernie Mac, Dave Chappelle, Steve Harvey, and Cheryl Underwood, just to name a small few. Besides the personalities he brought to light, this visionary was the brains behind the creation and marketing of the most iconic outlets and platforms for them to shine. *Def Comedy Jam*, Kings and Queens of Comedy Tours, and *Laff Mobb*. These platforms created a space where up-and-coming comedians of color, like myself, could test out material and make a name for themselves in the Black community. It's hard to believe, but even in the 1980s and 1990s, the well-known comedy clubs like Laugh Factory and places like that weren't trying to give Black comedians their due. When everybody started buzzing about the level of talent Bob was showcasing in all his different venues, he was able to create a powerful underground movement that eventually took over mainstream comedy. Yep, that's the Bob Sumner who I owe much of my career to!

I call this pivotal chapter "No Brakes," because I'm paying homage to how Bob and I had to roll and grind in order to get to where we sit today. There was nothing—nobody, no timing, no gig, no weather, no nothing—that could stop us from rolling. We literally lived life like a car with no brakes! Erratically careening from side-to-side, zigzagging from state to state, scraping guard rails—no brakes! Blowing at breakneck speed through red lights and rejections—no brakes! Fuck the caution lights and stop signs—no brakes! Oh, you don't see how we can do that? Okay, we'll show you—no brakes! They're only paying what for that gig? Okay, well you never know who might be there, I'll do it anyway—no brakes! The hustle was real and all roads were not lit with sunshine or paved with gold. We literally never stopped, oftentimes not even seeing the true payoff for the volume of effort we put in. That's the grimy, tedious, back-breaking, painful shit you never see once someone breaks through and succeeds. But, the one who succeeds never forgets.

Today, many young artists and creatives pack it all in after not having an immediate hit or payday. What we did, back in the days when we did it, was fueled by nothing but heart. You can only live this type of roller-coaster grind, you can't fake it. Toe-to-toe we blindly fought our way through and stuck to it long enough to tell the story of triumph on the other side. What Bob and I knew was that we were built to last and were going to figure out the game come hell or high water. Bob also knew how to read people like Miss fucking Cleo . . . call me now! I mean he could have a conversation with someone, or catch a specific facial gesture, and instantly know what they were all about. He is a straight-up no-nonsense O.G. who knows how to make connections that pay. He's masterfully skilled at putting parts together to create a mind-blowing sum total that nobody sees coming. He was a Seton Hall University cat. We clicked because I saw people like Bob growing up and honored their uncanny ability to make something out of nothing . . . he has that eye.

I could sit here all day long telling you about this inspirational behemoth, but nobody can tell you about the climate and culture I pieced my career together in better than Bob himself! So, if you pardon this interruption . . . let me introduce you to this mythological unicorn right now so he can fill in the blanks from his own point of view. Bob: the mic's hot and the stage is now yours!

* * *

Bob Sumner speaks . . .

Ah, man, thanks, Bill. I appreciate you too, my brother! Okay, here goes . . .

I know about these comedians and the struggle of wannabe funny men more than anybody. I mean, the shit nobody knows about them before they became the household names they are today. Besides knowing each of these giants' backstories, I was honored to have a front-row seat to live the experiences, hustle with them, and eventually watch them soar. Now, I've got nothing but mad respect and pride for comedians I've helped nurture and bring to the forefront.

The world needs funny men and women because it helps them face truths too painful to face soberly. Comedians are like the necessary chasers to your hardest, stiffest drinks. The ones that taste like acid going down, but if you put just a little bit of tonic or OJ in them they hit beautifully. That's what a skillful comedian does. They help people face the cold, hard facts about current affairs, cultural differences, all those landmine "isms": racism, sexism, capitalism, and all other hot-button topics. And, even more dope, they make people face the truth about themselves. You might not like it at first but no topic is off-limits for a really good comedian. That's the truth. When you can get people laughing about the uncomfortable stuff, you've also got a prime opportunity to get them thinking about reevaluating real world-changing shit as well. Comedians use their own pain to help audiences to cope with theirs. That's the transformational genius shit these magicians do. They wiggle their way in, cause you to let down your guard, and then WHAM! They get you right in the kisser without you even knowing.

Comedy is a tool that comedians use to figure shit out for themselves. It's self-healing; it's therapy. I love this stuff. I love the process because it's like medical science and religion all rolled into one. I enjoy finding talent and giving them the opportunity to fly. It feeds my soul and it makes the world a better place in my opinion.

Now that you know where my head is at, let's talk about Bill. Mr. Bill Bellamy came to me a while back saying he wanted me to do a "takeover" in the pages of this memoir. I had to scratch my damn bald head for a moment because I was trying to figure out what the hell he was talking about! A take-over? Is that some new age cyber shit? He then went on to describe his concept as somewhat of a record scratch moment, or an interruption. Like when the DJ used to scratch the record to get everyone's attention then make an announcement and start right back up again without missing a beat or changing the flow. When he put his vision like that, I finally understood what this brother was trying to say and I was touched.

There were things that I have talked to Bill about, or will talk about here, that no one else really knows. Bill and I have a running joke about "those ten dimes" from back in the days when we were broke like a motherfucker and down to count-ing our last ten dimes. Those last ten dimes kept us hungry, humble, and focused right up until this very day.

We get to a point in time with Bill and me, when we really decided that we were going for this comedy life, and we were going to crack the code together. Even today we're still riding together, even though professionally he does what he does, and I do what I do. Bill has his specific lane and I have mine, but somehow our roads always end up joining together and we collaborate on projects. Whenever he needs me, or whenever I need him, we're together. We've become more than business associates, we are family. All of my immediate family, are all close with Bill's family. His baby sister, Karen, and dearly de-parted brother, Julius, are like my kin. His mother, Edna, and father, big Bill, they're all my family. My mom and Bill's mom had some things in common too, like bingo and the lottery, and they loved to laugh and talk about their windfalls and adventures. Our bond is solid all the way around.

Big Bill and Edna always knew that I was there for their son all the way through and I'm still there. I start off laying all the cards on the table like this because it helps explain my life's mantra: I live by the concept of sowing and planting seeds everywhere I go. A farmer plants small, undeveloped seeds for a harvest. You don't know if or how well that seed is going to blossom, but you plant with faith. You don't know what your harvest is going to look like, how big, colorful, or bountiful the tree is going to be. We are all seeds planted with the expectation that we will flourish. On the flip side, we can all be farmers pouring faith and care into others.

I was from Seton Hall University, meeting a kid from Seton Hall Prep High School, who later matriculated to Rutgers University. Here you had two New Jersey kids who collided at a little comedy and jazz club I was trying to produce. I had a dream to create a place where young comedians, jazz artists, and everybody else who loved those two things could come together for fun and professional sport. The venue was called Terminal D in Newark, New Jersey. At Terminal D, we would have up-and-coming comedians, alongside some more established ones, testing out their material to see how it would play. I started to get into the comedy club game around 1985. In 1988 Bill had just graduated from Rutgers University and he visited the club. He got on the stage and for some reason, he got my attention. Mind you, we had so many different acts come through, but something about this kid made me sit up and take notice. You could tell he was still green, but he was polished at the same time. Bill went up there, and he was killing it! He even had something to say about the evening's host who no one ever messed with. I mean nobody fucked with this host, but he did. I was like damn! This dude's lightning quick on his feet. I didn't see it coming because he showed up looking all pulled together and smooth like an executive. I was loving everything about him and his delivery. He won me over from the jump.

As the comedy portion of the club started getting more popular than the jazz aspect, we changed the format entirely and it became just a comedy club. Not too long after, I had been thinking about leaving this room behind because I had outgrown it. Fresh out of college in the early 1980s, me and my friend Rocky Bryant, who's now the drummer for the Average White Band, had taken this room from being just an old-school strip club and turned it into something totally different, something more elevated. After it had gained popularity and tremendous buzz, the owners started to let the success get to their heads. They acted like they didn't need me involved anymore. After catching that message, I felt my work there was now done and I needed another challenge. My drive led me out of Terminal D, fueled by seeing Bill's potential and knowing he'd need a place to hone his skills. He was so promising that I knew I could bring him anywhere and create a buzz. I knew that there was a higher plane for us.

One particular night when Bill had wrapped his set at the club, I pulled him aside to have a conversation with him about our next steps. While we were talking, I noticed some guy was ice-grilling me from the other end of the bar. I mean he was really staring hard. Right in the middle of talking to Bill, I get out of my seat and I say to Bill, "Excuse me for a minute, let me go holla at someone." I made my way across to the other end of the bar where the guy was still staring me down. When I was squarely standing in front of him, I cocked my head to the side and said, "What the fuck you looking at me like that for, bro? What the fuck is going on? Do I know you?"

Just then Bill jumped up and came running over when he heard the commotion. He said loudly, "No, no, no! That's my man. That's my homeboy. He's cool. He's here with me!" You can't make this shit up. I was about to go off on this guy really bad. This was the first time Bill and I actually had an opportunity to sit down and talk and this craziness went down. I was about to clock his friend. That night, Bill saw another side of me. He saw I was no punk and that I wasn't afraid to handle business if I had to—no matter what was happening. And, just like that, I had won his respect.

That was the wacky beginning of my and Bill's formal working relationship. From there, he introduced me to Ron Workman, his best friend and college roommate, who later on became my Def Comedy Jam Tour road manager. Nobody knew I was getting ready to exit Terminal D. It was a shock to everyone because the place was thriving. I then set up shop at Club 88, with my partner Harold. We wanted the new venue to have a certain level of class so we had our sights set on Bill. At the time he was also holding down a day job at a tobacco company, delivering products to bodegas. The job came with a fucking station wagon and everything! He was set up. I remember Bill would show up to gigs with the back of the car stacked high with cartons of cigarettes.

I approached Bill's career like a serious brand. He was the total package and I knew that with the right management, exposure, and opportunities he was going to do big things. I started a management company called Ninth Avenue Management, with my friend Harold, to really formalize Bill's strategy. We went all in and had all sorts of branding stuff made: clocks, T-shirts, and flyers galore. All printed with Bill's face on them and ready to be distributed whenever and wherever. We treated him like a superstar long before he became one. We believed in him that much. My next-door neighbor was the road manager for the Manhattans and Regina Belle. Through this connection, we were able to get Bill to open up shows not only for them, but this also led to him being the opening act for Frankie Beverly and Maze and the O'Jays. His first major show was as the opening act for singer Brenda Russell, for whom I worked as a production assistant during that show. I also positioned him at this little spot in Linden, New Jersey, with a group called the New Style, who later became known as Naughty By Nature. I surrounded him with other talent that was also on the same path to make it to the next level; this created an undeniable buzz. In one career-making show at the Beacon Theater in New York City, Vaughn Harper, the popular charismatic voice of WBLS' *Quiet Storm* late-night radio show, told New York City that they're about to witness a rising star. Putting his stamp of approval on Bill he said, "Ladies and gentlemen, let me introduce you to Bill Bellamy, the next big thing!" We nearly lost our minds!

I was also known locally for my deejaying skills at comedy clubs. That's why a few years after I infused that element of Kid Capri into *Def Comedy Jam*. Bill became the host of this room at Club 88, and just like Harold and I predicted, the joint became the newest comedy hot spot. This instantly proved to me that I had an even bigger winner with Bill than I had realized. My back-end promotion skills and connections coupled with Bill's persona was a winning combination every time! We complemented each other well and handled our business.

Whether I had Bill flying out to Los Angeles to spend time doing the local comedy circuit, or make inroads with *Arsenio Hall Show* producers, which was a huge platform for young comics, Bill and I were on the 24-7 grind. The gigs kept coming and the audiences kept growing. We were manifesting our vision one engagement at a time.

While I was making changes to my new venue, I was still promoting jazz acts in different places. Now, here's a perfect example of the seed-planting analogy. One night I got a call from this lady, named Carmen Ashhurst, who was trying to get one of her jazz artists into the room that I was booking. At the time, I didn't have any room for him, but during my inquiries to other jazz venues I got wind of a jazz festival happening up in Ossining, New York. While speaking to the organizers, I suggested they should have my star comedian perform during the festival and they loved the idea. I was always pushing, trying to find ways to help Bill and expose his genius to as many people as I could. I knew in my soul he had that special star quality. We were on this ride together. That's how our "no brakes" life motto started. There were no brakes with what we were doing. It's like going down a hill, you step on the brakes and there are none. All you can do is put your head down, stay hyper-focused, and just keep going and going. No stopping for anyone!

Even though I couldn't get Carmen's act into my jazz room, I did get him on the roster to perform for the jazz festival in upstate New York along with Bill. During the event, we were chatting and Carmen was mentioning how much she liked Bill's performance. She then took out her business card and gave it to me. It said Def Jam Recordings on it. My mind started to race when I realized she wasn't just an artist's manager, she was actually the operations director. The name Def Jam was very impressive and influential and so was her role at the company. I was thinking maybe I could get Bill to open for some of their dope artists like LL Cool J and Public Enemy. I wanted to build a bridge any way I could. The only comedian they were using at the time was Chris Thomas from DC, who was called the mayor of BET's *Rap City*. I made a note to myself to call Carmen.

A few days after we got home from the jazz festival, I picked up the phone and started to plant the seeds at Def Jam Records with her. I started out with the usual small talk, "Hey, how you doing?"

Then bam, bam, bam! Right out the gate, she answers, "Guess what?"

"What?" I replied.

"I just got a promotion!" she announced as happy as can be. "I'm now the president of Def Jam Records!" She disclosed that she was looking for an assistant and asked if I knew anybody that would be interested.

Without missing a damn beat I replied, "You're talking to him right now!"

I now found myself on the inside track as the new assistant to the president of Def Jam Recordings. I was still on this comedy grind with Bill, but now I had greater leverage and credibility to throw behind it. One day I found myself in the conference room showing a demo tape of Bill. The footage was his performance at a *House Party* movie premiere event we did a few days earlier. Everyone was always curious about what I was doing on the comedy end of things and wanted to see the level of talent I had access to. At that time Russell Simmons partnered with film and movie producer/director Stan Lathan, deciding to join their empires. The next thing you know, *Def Comedy Jam* was born. I went from being Carmen's assistant to being vice president of talent for this new series. Now, that's how you reap your harvest!

Everything was finally coming together and all of the hard work was paying off. When I got the *Def Comedy Jam* show, I made Bill the show's poster child. I put together a special showcase at the Sweetwater Club in Manhattan to promote it all. The evening's jam-packed lineup included Chris Rock, along with rising stars Bernie Mac, Adele Givens, and Bill Bellamy. It was amazing and eventually created the roadmap for the *Def Comedy Jam* format. Which turned into the Def Comedy Jam Tour, which turned into everybody blowing up and getting their own individual deals. I was paying it forward and becoming a powerbroker in my own right. I was becoming hotter than fish grease.

You'd think that would be enough of a harvest, right? Well, Bill had more growing to do. The biggest seed was yet to bloom. I had Bernie Mac do his first live solo New York City performance at Bill's birthday party that I hosted. After that, Uptown Records had this thing called New York Live they hosted in Greenwich Village, a spin-off from R&B Live hosted in Los Angeles with Bill Hammond and Ramon Hervey. The New York version was produced by the late, great music exec Andre Harrell. Performers included Father MC, Heavy D, Christopher Williams, and a whole list of other names. We showed up wearing our *Def Comedy Jam* logo leather varsity jackets representing our new show. We were definitely the shit back then and everyone felt it. Everybody and their mother wanted a piece of the new show because it was so hot. Andre and my close friend Wendell Haskins, one of the producers, were visiting that evening as well. I told them that I had a comedian, who was the complete package, that I wanted to possibly host. I explained he was the perfect go-to host for what they were doing.

The gig came with no money. I think they offered him fifty dollars at the time to make the first appearance, but it wasn't about that. That night Jermaine Dupri's new group Kris Kross was debuting to a live audience. Bill came up on stage and literally shredded everyone with his jokes. He even had the damn balls to use Jermaine's group as the backbone of most of his set, poking fun at the way they wore their clothes backward. He was making shit up on the fly and landing every single joke like an atomic bomb. The next day, I got a phone call from a young lady, Tracey Jordan, who said that she was the vice president of talent at MTV. Tracey wanted to know how she could reach the guy who she saw perform last night at the New York Live event. She went on to say that she was getting ready to do a new show named *Fade to Black*, which eventually became *MTV Jams*, over at MTV and she wanted to see if Bill could do a couple of pilot episodes.

BOOM! And that's how the Bill Bellamy and MTV marriage was made. The rest is history!

Sometimes I was in the driver's seat, and sometimes I was in the passenger seat. Plenty of times we were both behind the damn car pushing it up the hill. But, at all times, every time, there were No Brakes!

Thanks for the memories, Bill. The best is yet to come. I love you, brother!

8

MESSY REALITY: SPRING BREAK AND THE BEACH HOUSE

"SMELLS LIKE TEEN SPIRIT"

Song by Nirvana

MTV always had a voyeuristic love affair with how young people moved about in the world. It was as much interest as it was a profitable obsession. This obsession also became their cash cow, and one that paid me well, so who am I to judge. The executives at the network loved seeing Gen X's raw energy, creativity, passion, and fuckups in full color. That's really why the network was created. It was conceived to put the lifestyle habits of that generation under a microscope to showcase what made them tick. In a lot of ways, MTV was the gatekeeper of youth. Older people (forties and beyond) secretly watched the channel to stay tethered to that raw energy even though they would outwardly pretend they didn't understand it. Young people watched because they felt understood and at home.

As I described in an earlier chapter, the way the MTV office was laid out screamed frat house. Young startup tech offices of today have nothing on the atmosphere that MTV created. There was a natural and authentic cool factor built in. MTV was the land of hair spray, cut-off shorts, Day-Glo everything, crop tops, and biker shorts. The network, and executives, knew how to create environments that drew youth in and made them want to stay to hang out. Places where they felt comfortable enough to lose all their inhibitions, letting just about everything all hang out, and I do mean "all-hang-out!"

This was a carefree but certainly not a mistake-free time. More importantly, these were the years right before the internet took over and changed the way we interacted with each other. Without the fear of having their wild night played back for everyone to see, young people behaved like young people. They weren't consumed with trying to one-up each other or ruled by the number of "likes" they could squeeze out of an event. Young folks in the 1990s knew how to live in the moment. That made them prime targets for the reality show circus. Naturally, MTV was the only one that could authentically draw them in and harness that magical energy.

I would say it slowly started to happen before their top-rated show *The Real World* first aired in 1992, but that one show kicked in the door for everything else. Whoever had the idea to throw a bunch of unsupervised horny twenty-plus-year-olds together in a cool-ass apartment and watch them self-destruct was an evil genius. Who needed writers and scripts when you had insecurities, four-letter words, raging hormones, and unlimited alcohol? Nature took over and it all unfolded for the world to see.

Based on the premise of watching animals at the zoo, these kids had no idea the magnitude of interest that would come their way. It was new, it was fresh, and human nature guaranteed that nobody would turn away from a train wreck. The show was a straight-up litmus test on society and a direct reflection of where we were at. No topic was off-limits: racism, sexism, homosexuality, transgender culture, anger management, narcissism, promiscuity, infidelity, venereal diseases. The list went on and on. And, from the beginning, it was piped directly into your living room for tens of millions of viewers to soak in. Even the format the show was filmed in was intentionally frenetic and home-movie-like. It resembled footage as if it was being captured by another house guest.

One socially charged issue that *The Real World* dove head-first into was HIV and AIDS. It was still a time when so much was unknown, and the virus was killing gay and straight people in huge numbers; everybody was scared. For most, the topic was still taboo, but not for MTV. They helped relieve the pressure valve by confronting the stigmas attached to the disease. They showed real dialogue and misinformation everyone in society was struggling with. It was a brave move, but this was the type of network they were. MTV was as unconventional and irreverent as its viewers.

If *The Real World* was there to subliminally study young people and what they struggled with on their path to adulthood, then their annual *MTV Spring Break* was pure unadulterated hedonism.

Let me frame this from my perspective for you. I am a Black man from a poor struggling Black family. We barely could afford school, and many of my friends and the teenagers I saw in my neighborhood were either pushing illegal rocks or baby carriages. It's just that simple. None of them were talking about hopping on a plane and going to Daytona Beach or Ft. Lauderdale, Florida, to celebrate midterms being over. We didn't have that luxury where I grew up. It was all hard work, pressure, and fucking life! Even though the concept of spring break was definitely foreign to me, I also found it intriguing. I could see why these kids got into it.

When I was asked to host *MTV Spring Break*, I had no idea what the hell they were talking about. It was billed as the ultimate kickoff party to summer for college coeds. Not only was it a wild weeklong beach party, it was also a full-blown concert with top artists catering to every genre of music. Even though the musical guests were diverse, I have to admit the thousands of kids that showed up were predominantly white, with just a few of us Black and Brown folks sprinkled in. Regardless of their ethnicity, they were all completely out of control. I mean crazy as fuck!

No matter what your flavor, or persuasion, there was a young lady at spring break that fit the bill. Short hair, long hair, blond, brunette, red hair; you name it, they were there for a wild time. It was the Ben and Jerry's of the dating pool and they traveled in party packs. On the flip side, there were guys that matched that Skittles mix as well. When I say "dating," I'm using the term very loosely because most of those kids were there for the great hook-up—think Tinder without having to swipe or geolocate. These girls were hot without even realizing what hot really was. A different type of organic attractiveness, unlike the hotness of today, which has become a calculated profession. Skimpy fluorescent bikinis and plenty of suntan lotion; it smelled like teen spirit for real! Basking under the sweltering hot Florida sun, these kids packed themselves in by the thousands, drunk on whatever cheap liquor, drug, or combination of both their allowance would buy. I did mention earlier it was wild, right?

When I say wild, I mean there were best bikini body contests, wet T-shirt competitions, crazy bets for even crazier stunts, whip cream, chugging tequila by the bottle, then puking in the sand. All of these antics gave viewers extreme shock value and a front-row seat. I'm sure if parents were sitting at home watching, they were horrified to see their college tuition money going down the drain. When I look back on it, through the politically correct filtered lens of today's social climate, that shit was bonkers. It was a literal PSA for sexual harassment televised for eight hours a day over the span of a week. The stuff those kids were doing in front of and behind the cameras would never fly today. As the father of a young lady who's college-age now, I cringe at the thought that Bailey would ever go to something like that. I know too damn much. What I also know is it would never happen. Sorry, Princess!

If one shitshow wasn't enough, I was tapped to host a spinoff special called *MTV Beach House* in Malibu, California. It was the West Coast Riviera of beach living. We filmed right off of the Pacific Coast Highway with the Pacific Ocean as our beach. They set us up in a cool-looking, weathered, pastel-colored beach house fully stocked with all the zany games, over-the-top blow-up toys, and floaties you could imagine. There were pillow fights among celebrities and plenty of kegs of beer on tap. What they should have provided in every room was Lysol, antiseptic wipes, and safe sex instructional videos! I sure hope that whoever owned the actual house never invested in a black light after we left. It would not have been pretty; shit was wild there too.

The program featured many of the same types of guest stars that *Spring Break* did and showcased the chill and wacky summer beach life vibe. I got to chat with folks like Radiohead, actors Rosie Perez, Jason Priestley, Pamela Anderson, 85 South, Dr. Dre, Snoop Dogg, and all the cool young stars of that time.

I realized early on at my MTV days that I could sit down at a table with anyone—Madonna, Sugar Ray, Michael Jackson, the Jonas Brothers, Nirvana—and they would all give me exactly what I came to get from them. Great content. People treated me like their funny cousin they loved to vibe with. This made me the ideal host, or camp counselor, for the weeklong bikini-fest. I knew how to make the crowd respond as the producers wanted them to. Fueled by their energy, I was just as stoked as the kids that came to hang out with us—rich white kids with a thirst for stardom and recklessness.

During that time, Grunge music had come out of nowhere, but it came in like a freaking rocket. Grunge was an iconic movement. It was something that most old folks, and definitely most Black folks, didn't understand. I was exposed to it all, but I can't forget the time when I interviewed Kurt Cobain on *MTV Beach House* right before his shocking suicide. I was stunned by his appearance. This guy was the rock star at the time and girls went crazy for him. Kurt showed up for the interview wearing skinny jeans, a striped sweater, and dirty Chucks. To add to his irresistible charm, the greasy fringe of hair that hung in his eyes moved every time he blinked. It distracted me so much during our interview because all I wanted to do was give him a bobby pin and ask him to pull it back. His disheveled appearance was jarring because I've always made sure to show up looking fresh, especially as a Black man. All I could think to myself was, Damn! These white kids get away with the most shit! And, bro, you need a shower! Besides his look, he was as cool as a motherfucker and didn't give a damn what I thought because he was a real-life fucking rock star!

Being able to engage and be socially curious was a skill most young people practiced before they got access to smartphones. Then technology put all of their friends and family at the tip of their fingers and they never had to look up from it to engage. My kids go to parties and just sit there on their phones the whole damn time, never looking up to chat with the people in the room. I wasn't making connections over text—I was sitting in a coffee shop and striking up conversations with people sitting next to me. You just had to be able to move through the world like that and connect with all kinds of different people.

Were the *MTV Spring Break* and *MTV Beach House* kids buck wild? Fuck yeah, but they were also active participants; not like the tech zombies of today. They were focused on living life in the present—hell, they were present! Well, most of the time, if they weren't plastered or high. The 1990s kids lived and had fun unapologetically. They were living life to experience it, not post it for bragging rights. To me, that's what you call living life with purpose. They were authentic and I miss that. On some level the world misses that too, but I don't think it's ever coming back. Thank goodness I had a VIP seat to what will go down in history as some of the most carefree times of our lives! If you ask me, the best experiences in life were meant to be private. Those crazy experiences and even crazier people made us all live like rock stars, even if only for a summer . . . It was everything. I finally understood what carefree living felt like and I must admit it felt damn good!

9

ROCK THE VOTE

"DON'T BELIEVE
THE HYPE"
Song by Public Enemy

Around 1992 when MTV decided to jump onboard the newly formed Rock the Vote coalition, created by former Virgin Music exec Jeff Ayeroff, they had no idea the seismic shift it would cause in celebrity culture, music, politics, and generations of young people. Politics would never be the same and neither would the degree of reverence given to the power young people wielded.

MTV may not have created the concept of Rock the Vote, but they did donate airtime and cultural clout to the cause. You have to remember that in those days MTV was the only platform for like-minded young people to converge. We were the social network of the 1990s and had the undivided attention of 60 million highly charged minds. For me, Rock the Vote was more of a movement than it was a platform. It showed the reach and influence MTV had in a very different way.

The network engaged superstars from every corner of the music industry to help. Rock stars like R.E.M., Madonna, Chuck D, and other entertainers were brought in to stimulate fans into action. Already having their respect and admiration, one word from them was all the spark needed to set the political scene ablaze. Through casual and quirky PSAs, which aired around the clock, these superstars encouraged fans to make themselves seen, heard, and felt by exercising their individual right to vote. Brilliantly, they empowered young people with breadcrumbs of facts, leaving them with a simple request to get involved.

Riveting televised town halls enabled the youth to have direct dialogue with politicians who were lobbying to get elected or reelected. That was unheard of. These teenagers (pimple-faced, shaggy-haired, and all) took command, rising to the occasion. Composed and collected, skillfully handling themselves in high-stakes venues, we had never seen this dynamic before. It was rattling. On the spot, they held lawmakers accountable where there had been no accountability. Politicians couldn't help but take these kids and their concerns seriously. They proved to be very formidable opponents.

Being one of the most recognizable faces at MTV, I was honored to be a vessel to help promote the Rock the Vote messaging. I was an influencer before the cultural term even existed and before people recognized they were being influenced. I'd never seen this level of fan engagement and trust me, I'd seen a lot.

Even though I went through the college system and graduated with pretty good grades myself, I was ignorant to how the political system truly worked. Yes, I learned the basics about the three branches of government, but it was taught in a very bland matter-of-fact way. Nothing about how they really interacted and impacted everyday folks' lives. What I mean is that ain't none of the information I learned was being connected to everyday movements. Nobody ever took the time to draw that dotted line back to why things showed up in my depressed little ghettoized neighborhood the way they did. Because it seemed so abstract, I sure as hell never retained that shit in my memory. I understood how money worked but didn't understand how it was allocated. For instance, I always assumed public schools had money to do everything they needed to do. It never dawned on me how dead wrong I was. As a grown man I now question if "the system" was ever meant for us to learn about the political process at all. Were they just teaching barebones basics to check a box, cover their asses, and move on?

Turns out, the biggest determining factor for school funding was the school's zip code—aka the demographics, aka the census. Now I got it! If you happened to live in a shitty district, then you were shit-out-of-luck. By actively participating in Rock the Vote, I started learning how certain districts got more funding appropriated than others. Another thing that blew my damn mind was how the Electoral College worked and the important stuff it prevented from working smoothly. What started out as just another work project became a lifelong educational experience. I was learning right along with the MTV audience, and it was empowering. If I thought I was smart before, learning the ins and outs of the political game made me feel more informed and even more powerful. Information is key.

Funding for neighborhood schools wasn't the only thing
that was determined by the district. Other resources including law enforcement, hospitals, and everything else associated
with the health and safety of a community were tied to it.
Due to creative redistricting and how money has been pushed
around, you got cops policing areas they have no connection
to or clue about. Back in the day, Officer Jones lived in your
area and played ball with people you knew. Officer Thompson
played football with your dad, and his father was a sergeant in
the force. What that meant was that you had law enforcement
cats that grew up in the neighborhood. They knew the pluses
and the minuses and could navigate around certain things that
outside cops couldn't. Growing up in the hood knowing we
had cops that we had a personal connection with kept a lot of
bad behavior in check. Then again, if you weren't really doing
shit, you wouldn't have to worry about it either.

Many cops that walk the beat in these depressed, predominantly Black and Brown neighborhoods of today live in white
neighborhoods. They are completely disconnected from what's
really going on in the streets they work in. You got guys, and
gals, around people they don't know and don't feel comfortable
around. That's when skittish quick-trigger behavior happens
because they have fear of the unknown. There's going to be an
energy of distrust happening, the guilty till proven innocent
kind of energy.

It doesn't have to be this way in these times. We have enough
intelligence and enough technology to know that all the stuff
we've been doing isn't working. Too many people, our Black
sons and daughters, are getting murdered for no goddamn reason. We know that police understand how to practice restraint.
We've seen them extend this "courtesy" to white perpetrators

of horrendous mass shootings. That's how you know they've got it in them when under pressure. Now, we just need to ensure the same level of care is applied across the board. Thanks to bodycam and cell phone videos the ugly truth is finally being exposed and revealed.

Back when I was younger, the inner workings of politics weren't something that was freely discussed in my household or neighborhood. To working-class folks busting their behinds just trying to put food on the table, politics seemed so remote, complicated, and not a priority. Without a bunch of education it was also probably intimidating to many.

One thing I was taught was how to act in interactions with the police. Sadly enough, every young Black boy and girl I knew was given the same talk. It was drummed into my head that the goal was to try to keep any contact with the cops at a calm level. No hothead stuff or spontaneous slick comments because the goal was to just get through the interaction alive. The teachings stuck with me and I sure as hell have passed them down to my own kids. Sadly, it's a part of their inheritance I wish I never had to bestow.

Until this day, even with my decades of fame and success, I always have my paperwork accessible to me when driving. I ain't got to be reaching for shit if I'm pulled over. I'm not doing none of that! If a cop pulls me over, I'm like this: "Here's my ID. I'm handing them over one, two. Yes, officer, how can I help you? What seems to be the problem, officer?" And yes, it's "yes, officer." This ain't no damn time to try and be funny or indignant. You will never hear of me going off like, "Why the fuck you pull me over?" Nope, not me. I'm going to be respectful right off the top. Sometimes that approach works, and sometimes it doesn't mean shit as Black people know all too well. All you can do is pray you ran into a good officer who's there to really serve, and most of all protect.

I'm taken back to 1995 when I bought my first Mercedes. It was the S500 AMG model, the big boy. I was feeling like King Kong that day. I swear to you, I had the car not even twenty-five minutes. I literally had just driven off the showroom floor and was on my way to pick up two of my friends I had called from my new car phone. I was showboating for sure. Cradling the phone on my shoulder and cheesing really hard, I announced, "Yo, this is Bill. I'm calling you from my brand-new Mercedes car phone, bro! I just rolled this bad boy off the lot and I'm on my way to pick you up to celebrate. Your boy just bought a brand-new Mercedes!" I proclaimed to them.

Man, as soon as I grabbed my boys and we turned back onto the main street, I heard the dreaded police siren behind me. In perfect unison, we all let out a drawn out, "Ohhh shiiittt!" To show you how crazy-conditioned we all were, the cops didn't say anything, and we all instinctively put our hands out the window. No joke. We literally rolled down all the windows and dangled our empty hands over the sides. Like clockwork, I was already prepared with my driver's license suspended from my fingers.

The white cop slowly walked up to the car and took my identification to examine it. His partner, who had made his way to the passenger side window, leaned in a little closer saying, "Yooooooo! That's my man Bill Bellamy from MTV!" He was barely able to contain his excitement and it instantly took the temperature down.

I politely chuckled and said, "Yes, officer, that's exactly who I am. What seems to be the problem?"

"Hey, Mr. Bellamy, I noticed that you were driving with

temporary plates and needed to pull you over to check it out. You know." He said this as the white cop craned his neck to peer inside my car trying to figure out what these young Black guys were doing in such an expensive ride.

"Well, officer, I have temporary plates because I just bought this car at the dealership and drove it off the lot. That's why." Now you know damn well what they really pulled me over for. The stereotype that nobody that young, or that Black, is driving this kind of car under legit circumstances. Yep, driving while Black! I am strictly legit playboy; always have been. You can take that to the damn bank!

In instances like this, I recognize the privilege of fame I benefit from, and I thank God for it. Even still, I cringe at how we always end up bearing the burden of suspicion and unwarranted fear. Not all situations end as mine did. Too many times even when Black folks say the right things and act respectfully, ignorance, prejudice, and abuse of power still win.

Jumping right into the middle of the controversial outcry to defund the police, I have to state upfront that I do not believe this is the right approach. Holding the rotten ones fully accountable is, however. I believe the disconnect comes from a lack of training. Just so there's no miscommunication here, let me clarify something. I do not believe you can train racism out of racist motherfucking KKK-type cops! I believe they purposely plant themselves in the force because they want to rule over Black and Brown folks and cause some harm. They need to just go. Take their guns, their badges, their Mace and kick their asses out! There is no place for that mentality in any police force. Especially when you are given the privilege of enforcing the law with deadly force—using my taxpayer dollars. I have no tolerance for that kind of cop.

The other larger majority of good-intentioned, poorly supported, and undertrained police can be supported and molded. I like the fact that I can call the police if there's a situation that gets out of control. Nine times out of ten they'll hopefully fix it without incident, just because they're the authorities. Cops have the ability to quickly change the vibe in an altercation, good and bad, and most sane people respond to that. They are there to help deescalate a lot of shit. I like having good police in our communities. We can't lose sight of the fact that there are plenty of good-hearted police officers still out there risking their lives to keep us safe.

During my Rock the Vote learning phase I inadvertently discovered that the government, or rather the people who run it, don't necessarily want you to understand what they're doing. Ignorance is as much a tool as it is a strategy. They don't want you to realize how important your vote is. Your vote is your voice. When people woke up and realized how the voting system was really set up to suppress certain communities' votes, all hell broke loose. Young people, of all colors, really started to realize how much it mattered, which led to an influx of voters the system couldn't account for. They were always there hiding in plain sight. They had just never been called on to show up before. Nobody had figured out how to speak directly to them. Once we did, that flipped the game.

Rock the Vote changed the landscape for young people, and it woke up tons of youth to the realization that this boring stuff that old white people were doing really mattered. It also taught them that politics determined their quality of life and the freedoms they enjoyed. MTV perfectly executed educating them on the importance of voting, activism, and political initiatives. We weren't preachy or judgmental in our approach and really came at it with the eyes of a teenager. We tackled micro issues youth could grasp and assemble around. Unknowingly, we were directly affecting the future livelihoods and aspirations of the next generation. MTV made politics cool.

As a part of the Rock the Vote campaign, fellow VJ Kennedy and I were flown to Washington, DC, to cover the political conventions. I reported on the Democratic one and Kennedy handled the reporting from the Republican Convention, which aligned more closely with her own personal political bent. We each had a blast, and it was a cool experience to be immersed in. We were right there on the convention floor rubbing elbows with the lawmakers, getting in their faces and asking questions that our young viewers wanted to know. I remember that was the first time I met President Bill Clinton. He was the right president at the right time for this initiative. He became a rock star in his own right. Young people loved him because he was relatable and not removed like others before him. His charisma made him perfect for that initiative.

My presence at events like this was a reminder of what learning and evolution looked like in real time. I would ask off-the-wall questions to these young politicians during interviews. I'd ask things like, "What would make you want to be a congressman or senator? I never met anybody in my neighborhood who said they were running for the Senate. This sounds like you're getting in a spaceship or something. Or like you want to be a damn astronaut!" They'd laugh and then fill me in on their process or journey to a life in politics.

Regardless of the subject of my interview, my approach was always meant to catch people off guard by doing the unexpected. I was genuinely amazed at how different being a politician was from the normal kind of aspiration people had where I came from. In reality, and because of the impact these cats had on ghettos, we all should have been striving for that title. What I eventually realized was that if you are not acclimated to the world of politics, it's like learning a different language entirely. It has its own ecosystem.

Knowledge breeds confidence. The confidence to use your voice and share it with conviction. The sureness to lean into that knowledge, using it to influence and enlighten others. Historical figures such as Fred Hampton, Angela Davis, Rosa Parks, and Shirley Chisholm have always been influential to the Black community. The church also churned out some of the most prolific voices in civil rights we still revere. Reverends Martin Luther King Jr., Malcolm X, Jesse L. Jackson, and Al Sharpton each created invaluable building blocks for generations of young people to learn from. Reverend Jesse L. Jackson's audacious presidential run in 1984 and his Rainbow Coalition platform stood on the shoulders of Fred Hampton's similar message from decades prior. Creating waves in Black and Brown communities was always a goal of past generations' trailblazers; they just never had access to a behemoth platform like MTV. Can you imagine if they had?

New political voices of color like Vice President Kamala Harris, Senator Cory Booker, Congresswoman Alexandria Ocasio-Cortez (AOC), Representative Val Demings, Senator Raphael Warnock, and Stacey Abrams have stepped in as voices for a new generation. So did Hall of Fame sports icons like baseball phenom Jackie Robinson, football legend Jim Brown, and basketball trailblazer Kareem Abdul-Jabbar. Present-day influencers like Allen Iverson refused to show up as anyone but their authentic self. LeBron James, Carmelo Anthony, and Colin Kaepernick have all brilliantly used their amplified voices to inform and empower the people: our people. For me, being a beacon of light to move young people to learn and become active participants in their future added great purpose and perspective to my life.

These were the principles that President Obama grew up under and that's why he was so successful and transformational to the political system. He went back to the grassroots blueprint, using the technology as a primary mechanism to reach the young and restless, much like MTV was used in its time. While the old-school establishment was relying on predictable methods, Mr. Obama reverse engineered old-school tactics of taking it to the streets across color lines. Unexpectedly, he also sprinkled in new-school technologies to amplify the ask. Droves of passionate street teams, coupled with aggressive small incremental fundraising on social media, made him unstoppable. Two dollars, five dollars, ten dollars, it all counted and made people (all people) feel like they had skin in the game. He made his contributors feel like they mattered. The old guard didn't see President Obama or his intelligent approach to fundraising coming. It was a beautiful thing to see a Black man, of humble beginnings, outsmart "the system" designed to discard people that looked like him.

My political enlightenment has given me more things to talk about in comedy. It has deepened my level of material and challenged me to leave my audiences with a little more food for thought. You can only talk about what you know. Exposure to different things allows you to share acquired knowledge. Proudly I have grown exponentially. I will never ever forget the first time I met President Obama. I was a guest at a big political fundraiser he was having in Los Angeles. This is how goofy I can be. I was standing there in a circle of folks having a conversation when I heard this familiar voice behind me say, "How are you doing, Bill?"

I turned around and found myself face-to-face with the president of the United States of America. Stone-faced Secret Service men crowded all around him and all conversation in the circle had stopped on a dime. In true wisecracking style, I answered, "How do you know my name?"

Instantly a huge grin came across his face as he said with that familiar chuckle, "So, Bill, you don't think I have cable? You don't think I watch TV? You don't think I love comedians too?"

I was kind of stunned because I was only half-joking when I asked how he knew my name. I was staring at the president and all I could think to myself was, You bullshitting! You just said my goddamn name! I fanned the fuck out! It was a seminal moment realizing that this powerful pillar of the world actually knew who Bill Bellamy was. Me, little old me. Damn, I had come a long way!

Years before this encounter, I was in New York City when President Obama first won. I will never forget the moment. This is the first, and only, time in my life where I felt like everybody came together. For about twenty-four hours it miraculously felt like this country had no racism. Everybody in New York was in the middle of Broadway, crying, hugging, and screaming, "We did it. We did it. We did it. Oh my God!" It was the use of the word "we" that struck me. In that brief shining moment, I got a glimpse of what the world could look like if we saw ourselves in each other. I was crying for many of the same reasons too. All I could think was, Yo, this is crazy. My grandparents would never believe this! They fought so damn hard just for the right to vote. Now, there's a Black man running the country!

A cool Black dude too. So many emotions overtook me in that moment.

During his inauguration in Washington, DC, my wife, Kristen, and I attended. It was bone-chillingly cold sitting out there waiting for the ceremony to unfold. Noses running, tears flowing, and we were all joyfully packed in to witness history in the making. As far as your eyes could see, every corner of the city was overflowing with human bodies of all ethnic backgrounds. It was like a true gathering of the United Nations. What a beautiful sight to behold! Everybody was so courteous and you could feel that this wasn't just any old inauguration ceremony. It was like a movement. An important moment in time. After witnessing these two events firsthand, it made me realize that this country, this world, really can be changed through the power of the people. Every single vote really does count, if you are committed enough to cast it. If you push hard enough and long enough, you can make a change. That's why my wife and I stay committed and active politically. To this day we encourage people to vote, get informed, and seek the knowledge they need about what's going on in their communities. Information is key.

Today Black folks, and primarily Black women, are controlling the narrative. It's something that has never happened before. Vice President Kamala Harris, who I've known for many years, is proof positive of this shift. The first female vice president is an HBCU sistah! Let that one sink in. Not forgetting about Stacey Abrams from Georgia who is a full-throttle pioneer at galvanizing the support of the underrepresented. She's a perpetual thorn in the side of all Republicans and I love her tenacity. Stacey single-handedly flipped Georgia for the Democrats. Outwitted all the naysayers and turned that state upside down. Her relentless protection of equality in voting accessibility for communities of color changed the political landscape forever. It gave all of them Republicans the blues! These are our communities' new superheroes. I couldn't be prouder to lend my influence to the cause. I still work constantly to raise money and awareness for voices and platforms I believe in.

Once your eyes are open you can never shut them again. I will never be the type of guy who just shuts up and dribbles! In all reality, what great nation can stand, or thrive, without the voices of all their people represented? Power to the people.

10

Y2K BOOM AND BUST

"WHOOMP, THERE IT IS"

Song by Tag Team

Fuck Napster! Fuck Napster! Fuckity-Fuck Napster!

I could end this chapter right here and feel like I've said all I needed to say about the music-sharing platform. In a nutshell, it was a bullshit internet software that came on the scene ruining everything for everyone. I'm not going to lie . . . I wish I had thought of it. I'd be retired right now on my own private island, sipping Jamaican rum punch for breakfast, lunch, and dinner. If you were around to live it, you probably already know how catastrophic the Napster platform was to the music world. If you weren't, here's a bit of context around why artists no longer make money selling their music.

For those of you who were born after 1995, here's a shocking PSA for you. We used to have to look shit up in books and encyclopedias! The internet wasn't always a thing, and everyone used to have to practice patience for everything else. And, the universe still functioned just fine. There was this wonderful feeling called anticipation when I knew my favorite artist's album was about to drop. Before Napster, people watched their favorite music station on television and saw a video. If you liked the video, it compelled you to go to the record store and buy the album or CD. Let me emphasize, did you hear me when I said I had to go to a record store to get my music? I was literally just like an excited little kid planning out my trip as if it were a damn birthday party. These were "the feels" you got no matter how many albums you splurged on in a year. The joy was just as much about the lead-up as it was about the purchase. Worse if it was a double CD drop, like Michael, Janet, Madonna, and Tupac used to do. I'd be losing my goddamn mind spending two to three hours in Tower Records just listening to new releases like it was a drug I couldn't get enough of. Ah, those were the good old days.

Very few artists owned their music or held the rights to their masters at that time. Unknowingly, young artists were signing a bunch of bad contracts that held them captive and in bed with the record labels on every single level. For instance, let's say that as a new artist you signed a million-dollar deal with the promise of delivering three albums to the label. That million dollars didn't go into the artist's pocket, despite what the media reported. You owed all of that money to the label. The deal was set up like a bank-type loan. Getting a record contract was like signing with a bank to produce your record!

On top of that, every limo ride, every hotel room, every damn thing was accounted for. The labels made sure artists had a company credit card to charge all of their expenses to.

No, they weren't just being considerate or trying to make your life easier. It was somebody's job to run behind the talent keeping tabs on every dollar that he/she/they spent. Wasted studio time—there was a cost for that. Lavish meals, lawyers, press agents, hair, makeup, clothing, stylists—it all got billed back to the talent. They fronted you the million dollars to produce the albums, but they needed to recoup their costs before any artist saw a damn dime in payment! Some artists were savvy enough to negotiate royalties on the back end; others weren't. By the time they saw their money as an artist, it was a minuscule fraction of the original amount. Everyone else had already filled their bellies, and the talent was left with the scraps. Only the literal carcass because the buzzards had already swooped in.

From what I remember, Michael Jackson was probably one of the few artists whose record deals paid him in the dollar figure per album sold. For argument's sake, if a Michael Jackson CD cost the consumer fourteen dollars, then Mike probably made one dollar per CD sold. Believe it or not, that kind of compensation structure was unheard of! Most artists were getting like twenty or twenty-five cents per album and shit like that. That's how bands like TLC went broke back in the day. Their contract terms on paper were garbage, and their royalty agreement structure was also extremely weak. Mind you, this was all done intentionally because labels knew that young artists didn't know their true worth and they were desperate for a deal—any deal. To top it all off, artists like TLC were spending lots of money to keep up their public image because they had to. Public perception is what fanned the flames of popularity, album sales, and longevity in the music business. It costs plenty of cash to be a top musician. Then, if you were part of an ensemble, that money got diced up in so many additional ways. If I were a betting man, I'd put my money on that being one of the reasons why Michael Jackson probably made the decision to go solo and leave his brothers. Everybody was in his pockets, and it probably seemed like he was working for free being one of the Jackson 5.

MTV's core purpose was to drive the promotion of artists' work. The network was also there to build relationships with them so they could capture and narrate their careers as they unfolded. Our formula worked brilliantly. We helped craft and sell the persona of artists in a video diary for the world to see. VJs built an imaginary bridge between the artist and their global audience. And, when they didn't have an established audience yet, they came to us so we could introduce them to the world. Additionally, MTV's presence allowed record companies to methodically control the narrative around record releases. In 1994 when Napster came out of nowhere, it was like an ominous alarm went off across the music world. Everything was up for grabs—no holds barred.

Everybody who worked in the music business in the 1990s was classified as a hot, young record executive on the rise. Opportunities were everywhere you turned. Everybody wanted to be in the business; I mean it was hotter than Arizona in the summertime. All my friends were either corporate attorneys, artist representatives (A&R) for labels, or marketing executives and talent scouts. It was probably one of the most amazing industries to be in as a young person because age wasn't a predictor of how much money you could make. A young person at a label could be well into the six-figure income range at just twenty-four or twenty-five years old. This was in the 1990s when that money stretched really far. If you knew the value you brought to a label and could prove it, you were given more responsibilities—the money inevitably followed. If a person was ambitious and willing to work, where they started didn't have anything to do with where they finished. You could come in as the coffee guy, and in one year get a promotion to head up the jazz division. Smaller labels were as much into developing music executives as they were into developing singing artists.

There was nothing but crazy mad money flowing and huge expense accounts to go wild with. Def Jam, Arista, Jive Records, and Island Records were powerful independent labels churning out superstar after superstar and always on the lookout for the next best thing. Young cats coming up like Craig Kallman, Damon Dash, Lyor Cohen, Puffy, and Russell Simmons all had that fiercely competitive entrepreneurial fire. They were the brazen cultural ambassadors that fueled the music business of that time. They operated on unfiltered gut instincts and kept a ton of money flowing—across the board. There were no ceilings on that shit.

Everybody started scrambling after Napster started to gain a foothold. Music executives looked at each other, scratching their balls, saying, "Yo, what the fuck is this?"

After Napster exploded, slowly many of my friends started losing their high-level industry jobs. It was whack. They went from wining and dining business associates to absolutely no expense accounts, or ones that were heavily scrutinized. From buying houses and fly-ass cars, straight to the unemployment line, struggling to pay rent. It all happened so damn fast. Labels began cutting back mercilessly because all the revenue they once had from sales wasn't coming in anymore. Consumers abandoned purchasing and started sharing music.

MTV always understood that our young audience craved

cutting-edge trends. As a new network, years prior we capitalized on their ability to turn on a dime and be rebellious. By nature, teenagers hated rules, and we banked on that! The very premise that Napster was built on was right up their alley, but we didn't see it coming.

Napster came in and said their users didn't have to buy the music they were listening to. Adding insult to injury, users could easily share curated lists of songs with as many friends as they wanted—for free! All this without leaving their damn couch!

The record companies went ape shit! Now the economy of record stores, signing new artists to deals, and publishing were all jeopardized by one piece of technology. Because Napster was based on file sharing, they got around the antiquated laws against pirating. "Technically" what their users were doing wasn't considered stealing; they were just passing it around. Everyone who made a dollar in the music business hated Napster! I mean everyone, except the geek who created the shit and those who benefited. I'm sure he banked big money off advertisers wanting to get a piece of the audience he was pulling. Even though we hated it, and could see the destructive pathway it was creating, we couldn't ignore it because our audience was hooked. All I know is that the shit would clog up your fucking computer!

Without question the new streaming platform killed us. It devoured everything and everyone in its wake. The part of Napster I hated the most was that it devalued the artist. It devalued all of the long hours and hard work in the studio collaborating with writers, producers, sound engineers, and art designers. Napster cheapened it all.

The sheer pace of the industry changed overnight. Everything sped up and artists became disposable one-hit-wonders

like never before. Forget the flavor of the month, how about
the flavor of the day? Artists woke up to the hustle and
stopped chasing traditional record deals. If they were smart,
they sought out distribution deals with labels instead. Under
those new types of arrangements, talent produced their own
shit and only relied on the record labels to get the finished
product out to market. The two major differences were who
owned the material and who allocated the share of percentages
from sales. Artists reclaimed ownership of their intellectual
property. The hand that rocks the cradle shit!

Napster paved the way for other platforms like Apple Music.
Even though I'm a nostalgic type of cat, I must confess, I haven't
bought a full album in years. Now you can listen to artists'
work without spending a dime. Or, if you buy a package, you
get x-number of songs and can listen to every album in the
world. Consumers took on the mindset of, Why do you need to
be loyal to one artist? You can cherry-pick three songs on one
album and throw the other ones you don't like right back.

Being knowledgeable about the artist's creative process, I
understood that albums used to be arranged like a book. Each
song signified a different chapter to the whole body of work.
When you reached the end of the album, that's when the full
story unfolded. There was a beginning, middle, and end. These
platforms have stolen our ability to give music a chance; to give
artists a chance to grow into their style. That's why all the damn
music sounds the same now. Nobody wants to take a risk. The
process of developing new artists is now like a Krispy Kreme
donut conveyor belt just waiting for the red light to come on.

How do artists make money today? Concerts, lucrative
branding deals, or Las Vegas residencies. They've diversified
their portfolios; they had no other option.

Independent labels weren't able to recover or survive. What started happening was those smaller operations started to get gobbled up just like Pac Man. Universal Music Group, one of the main culprits, started snatching labels—whoosh, whoosh, whoosh—and brought them under one umbrella, giving birth to the big corporate label. Even though artists would still say they got a contract under the smaller label name, they were actually operating under the thumb of the larger corporate entity. It was similar to when Apple came into the tech space, grabbed all the apples, and left the playground.

Consolidation of people came next. The bigwigs brought in their own executives and A&R people. They knew how to crunch numbers but didn't understand the flavor that moved the culture. Extremely talented artists had their projects overlooked or pushed to the back burner. Now, they were sitting on the bench for three, four years growing more and more bitter and disinterested in the craft.

MTV had wisely made the pivot to producing reality TV in the early part of the 1990s. And, the rest is history on that trailblazing front. Three words for you: *The Real World!*

Did I see the handwriting on the wall and begin to plot my next act? You're damn right I did! Remember, I saw where the MTV game started. I knew that with the introduction of Napster, the influence, access, and power we would carry in the future was questionable at best. Our audiences also didn't need us in the same way anymore. If artists like Janet and Madonna were feeling it in their pockets, you know MTV started to see it in our ratings. Once again, it was time to spread my wings and fly. The party was officially over.

We lost the essence of the music with Napster. Social platforms are now distribution mechanisms and A&R pipelines. Everybody's on TikTok, Snapchat, Instagram, YouTube, Only Fans, slinging exclusive content. And, everybody's a singer/superstar artist because they can brag about their followers. Early in my career, when I was grinding from gig to gig, you had to earn those types of accolades. Artists had to earn their street cred. Social media and technology stole the mystique of what it means to be an artist. We relinquished one thing to gain another. Outside the obvious convenience of lightning-quick distribution that Napster opened up, no platform ever figured out how to keep the value of the purchase alive. Mindlessly downloading music now means the purchaser feels no significance behind their purchases. It's automated to the max and feeds off robotic behavior. You don't even have to actively whip out cash or an actual credit card anymore; it's all stored in the cloud for you. No waiting, no anticipation, no butterflies, no nothing! Napster created that monster in my opinion. With just one small idea, the internet was the rise and fall of the music business. It was a grenade in the hole! The Godzilla that trampled over everyone.

The industry may have changed, but music will always be the pulse of our culture. It will always capture what people are feeling, learning, and struggling with. No computer platform can ever delete that. Long live music!

11

THE BIG MOVE: GOING HOLLYWOOD

———

"GOING BACK TO CALI"

Song by the Notorious B.I.G.

I was about seven years into my stint at MTV when I started getting that gut feeling I needed to move on. MTV was never interested in promoting me as an individual. I looked around and realized no one was going anywhere, definitely not to the movies, which is where I wanted to be. The other personalities and VJs were getting frozen in the MTV world. They were content to keep being the ones doing the interviewing. I wanted to be the one getting interviewed! I hired a publicist and started to get myself out there more. After all, I was in the Bill Bellamy business. I remember reading an ad for a movie that was looking for a "Bill Bellamy type." I'll be damned! I never realized

I was a type. I finally knew I needed to spread my wings and fly the coop.

My manager at the time, Ron Workman (aka "Work"), shared a conversation with me that he had with an advertising guy at MTV. They were casually chatting about where the channel was heading and projects on the horizon. You see, Ron was super business-minded and always kept me focused on what made the wheels churn when it came to back-end productions. He knew that things ran in cycles and you always had to stay ahead of the wave so that you didn't get swallowed by it. Ron had commented to the advertising executive that he noticed MTV was moving in the direction of programming much more reality and unscripted formats. It was obvious they were drifting away from music video–themed shows. The ad guy replied, "Ron, this era of music programming is going to be over. We have to start making more money and videos just don't bring in big money anymore. We need more breaks to attract commercial ad spots. That's where the money is at. We're going to be bringing in all-new shows to get sponsors and commercials. Videos are going to be pushed to the back. That's the truth."

It was tough to give up that everyday access and exposure to reaching fans, but you can't be a movie star and be an on-air personality for MTV. I was watching people around me blow up—Chris Tucker, Martin Lawrence, Jamie Foxx, and Will Smith. Just blow up! I wanted some of that. I was ready to make that transition. I knew my career had another level to reach. I was bringing it to the entertainment business; I'm a hustler. I said to myself, I'm going to hustle them and make them comfortable in thinking they're hustling me.

I knew how Hollywood people thought. I knew what producers and directors wanted. If they wanted me to be a little more charming and colorful so we didn't "frighten" anybody or ruffle any feathers, I'd give them that side of me. Bam! If someone wanted me to be over here and do this game-show-guy routine, I can switch it up and give them that. If they wanted me to play in a movie and be a little grimier? Boom! I could give them hard and grimy too. If my life had taught me anything, it taught me that there was nothing I couldn't do. I was tired of interviewing A-list actors like Halle Berry, Salma Hayek, Tom Cruise, and Keanu Reeves, asking them what it took for them to succeed. I knew what it took. I just needed to get my ass out there and do it. Hollywood was calling my name because it represented unlimited possibilities. I was ready to pull out all the stops. It was time to reactivate the no brakes grind mode.

In 1998, Ron and I officially decided it was time to cash in our chips, bite the bullet, and commit to the goal of me becoming a full-fledged movie star. Taking my television career to the international IMAX-screen level. We packed up and moved from New Jersey to Los Angeles to take on Hollywood. All systems go!

Now that we were physically based where movies were being created, it was time to dig in and make that shit happen. MTV opened the doors to everything for me. During my time there I was dabbling in acting and had a good run of success with it. You do remember the iconic Black story called *Love Jones*? That was Larenz Tate, Nia Long, Isaiah Washington, and me in 1997 planting our flag in Hollywood. It was my first real crack at a dramatic-type role. It was your typical boy meets girl story told through the lens of young, ambitious, and upwardly mobile Black twentysomethings.

Hollywood, my character's name, couldn't have been more of the stereotypical Hollywood jerk. Brash and devious, completely opposite from what I have patterned my life after. The dude was scripted to be a straight-up hater who was hated for being a complete sabotage artist. Even though he was different from me, I didn't have to dig too deep to get his essence right. I grew up with cats like him. Cats you wouldn't leave your girl, or wallet, alone in a room with but deep down you knew that if shit really went down, they'd have your back in a New York minute. Hollywood was a jealous bastard and I nailed it!

The funny thing about *Love Jones* is that before the movie even existed, I told Nia Long in an *MTV Jams* interview that I was going to do a movie with her. True story. Staring at her perfect, creamy chocolate brown complexion, cute little haircut, and killer dimples, I was giddy. Her smile was magnetic. I was just throwing it out there because we had spontaneous chemistry during the interview and it felt right. I could see us using our natural vibe to make a great film. Wouldn't you know it, not even a year later, Nia and I were sitting in a scene together for *Love Jones*. In between takes I turned to her and said, "Do you remember when I predicted this?"

She answered, "Oh my God, Bill, I was just sitting here thinking the same thing." I guess that's what it means to manifest shit.

Then in 1997 came one of my favorite roles I've played to this day. I played the lead character named Drayton Jackson, or Dre as his friends called him, in *How to Be a Player*. This movie was pure slick style and a comedic guide for guys trying to live on the edge, juggling multiple ladies at the same time. It was like my Booty Call joke played out on film. The fun part about the character is that Dre wasn't arrogant or disrespectful, he just loved playing that romantic chess game. He wasn't shy about using his looks or personality to get out of predicaments. Dre was a fool for sure. He orchestrated the wildest scenarios and talked the most crap to butter up these ladies and play his games. No harm meant though, this dude was pure alpha energy on crack. Especially because he never got caught in his twisted lies. Who wouldn't love that? I was like a kid in a candy store playing that role and had a blast with it. The cool thing about the movie is that men loved it because, of course, they wished they could be him. But women also loved it too, because the storyline was fun and lighthearted, not mean-spirited. Dre bit off more than he could chew with his love interests and was always hilariously struggling to make his messy situation work. Just when his back was up against the wall, he'd adapt on the spot. Dre would flirt like hell with drama but didn't panic when the drama came knocking at his door. His hustler would kick in and he'd start placing these chicks strategically so they never ran into each other. He was that evil genius motherfucker you wanted to hate, but he showed up cool as a cucumber just like Billy D. Williams, so you couldn't hate him. So many dudes to this day come up to me like, "Man, you know boss, I was watching that *How to Be a Player* joint last night. You're a straight O.G.! You taught us that game, playa!"

It cracks me up every time because I always end up saying to them, "You know that movie ain't real right? Ain't nobody getting away with shit nowadays. Not with social media!"

Things were on fire in my movie career and I was hitting on all cylinders. Back-to-back films that did well at the box office. Growing chatter about my acting ability and the characters I was playing. The phone was ringing constantly with people wanting to include me in their projects. It was a good time, a promising time. I was that guy. The likable Black guy everybody could relate to. The guys liked me because I wasn't standoffish or pompous. They wanted to be smooth and dress like me, leading with their charisma and charm. That whole persona was Bill Bellamy the comic. I had busted my ass for years perfecting it so that I could attract the audiences. To see that I had made that kind of impact was flattering for sure.

My first major big-budget movie was 1999's *Any Given Sunday*. It was an Oliver Stone movie, so you know all the stops would be pulled to make it a success. Big production value, top-shelf talent, huge and wide promotion strategy. These were all the missing elements that smaller Black movies, at that time, didn't have access to. Going into the movie I had high hopes that this would be my springboard into other major leading-man roles.

I knew I was going to be auditioning for the part of a wide receiver on the team, so Ron had me out on the field training hard for the part. When I showed up for the actual audition, we wanted everything to be natural and authentic. I tapped into my athletic roots and we dug in, throwing the ball constantly and doing training camp sort of drills in preparation.

Before I was officially cast, Oliver Stone held an open call workout at the University of Southern California (USC) campus. Mind you, this was my first time experiencing what it was like to be around a huge production setting, so we showed up extra early to get in some more practice time. The nerves were on full-scale alert. We showed up looking official. Sponsored from head to toe, representing in our Reebok gear. Every Black actor in Hollywood was at that audition. They were there to either try out for the running back role that LL Cool J eventually got or the wide receiver role that I was auditioning for. On the field, there were three huge tents set up, and when we went into the first one, our eyes nearly popped out of our heads. They had three chefs cooking breakfast and a massive spread of all types of food beautifully displayed. That right there let us know this was not a regular audition.

Guess who was originally cast to play third-string quarterback in the movie? It was P. Diddy, who was dating Jennifer Lopez because she rolled up to the audition that day with him. I've got mad love for Puff and his talent as a musician and actor, but when I was watching him practice that day, I could instantly tell that athleticism was not his strong suit. It was clearly challenging for him to throw the football forty yards. I believe it was in part due to his "athleticism" and the other part due to a really bad hand injury he sustained before the movie started filming. To top it all off, he jammed his finger on one of the damn plays. That was it for him because right after that, he left early and called it a wrap. From what I could tell, featuring him in the quarterback role was going to be a hard one to sell.

The story that circulated about one of the reasons behind why Puffy got taken off the project and Jamie Foxx got put in was a little bit crazy. Apparently, one day Puffy was doing a table read of the script with Al Pacino and Oliver Stone, but his cell phone kept blowing up. Rumor has it, he refused to turn it off. Supposedly it rang one too many times for Al Pacino, who looked at Oliver Stone and laid down the law. Allegedly, Pacino gave Oliver an ultimatum saying something like, "It's either him or me. I won't work like this!" Well, we know who won that battle. Now, I can't confirm that this was the only reason Puffy and Oliver parted company on the film, but I'm sure that if it went down like I'd heard, it couldn't have helped.

When I heard the play by play, I said to myself, Now, you're in the room with Al Pacino and Oliver Stone (two of the biggest goddamn names in Hollywood), and you can't shut it down for two hours? Damn, that right there is some crazy stuff. Better him than me!

I busted my butt during the audition and got cast in the role of Jimmy Sanderson, a wide receiver on the team led by Al Pacino who played the veteran coach. If you know anything about the genius of Oliver Stone, then you're familiar with the fact that he shoots a ton of scenes. I think the original time stamp on *Any Given Sunday* was over four hours. He went deep into developing each character's narrative arch. My character had plenty of scenes and a full parallel storyline, as did LL Cool J's character. It was fantastic! The reality is, however, no film is going to market being that long. That's where the cutting room floor comes in and that bitch is brutal. Unfortunately, that's where most of my scenes ended up and my life-changing beefy role ended up being reduced, which was painful. That's the movie business for you.

If I didn't admit my disappointment in how this went down, I'd be lying to you and myself. I was pissed, but there was nobody to blame. Nobody to be pissed at. This was just how the business of filmmaking operated. My team was as shocked as I was because they knew the kind of work I put in. Oliver Stone wrote me a personal letter and thanked me for bringing such raw emotion to his film. He shared that some of my biggest scenes had to be edited to keep the length tight. That was a nice touch because I know he wasn't obligated to explain shit to me. Lesson learned.

Hollywood can be tricky and it's completely driven by timing and relationships. It's a bit of a numbers game ruled by luck. You have to keep turning out back-to-back box office hits to stay relevant in the business. Saturating the market with your face to remain relevant is what keeps people talking about you. Why do you think once an actor has even one major role you quickly hear they're doing five or six more behind it? Their agents wisely know they may only get that one sliver of spotlight to shine, that's why they run headlong into it. As time moved along, and the internet cranked it up to lightning speed, people in power at the studios moved around even more quickly. Executives I had worked and built relationships with had moved on. The kids that I had grown up with on MTV were now having kids of their own. I was stuck between that new younger generation who only knew MTV for their zany reality shows, not music videos, and those who were now focused on building careers of their own.

Then there was the elephant in the room: being a Black actor. There were only so many leading-man roles given to us. It was tough, to say the least, and very hard to wrap my mind and ego around. The competition was fierce! I have always been sharp when it comes to reading trends, so while I still kept the door open on acting, the reality was that bills had to be paid too. I also had a new wife to support and a growing family. My life was changing.

I've never been one to get a swollen head. I've always taken my fame in stride and tried not to lose sight of who I am or where I came from. Because nothing was ever given to me easily, I've always remembered that at any moment, shit can all change. The ability to pivot and adapt has always been my ace in the hole. Turning negatives into positives is what I have done my whole life—right from the very start. I've approached my career as a business first, fame later.

The business-minded side of me said to get back out there

and go hard with my comedy again until I got the role that was going to put me on IMAX screens. That's exactly what I did. I hit the road again and did my shows to sell-out audiences. After all, I will always be a comedian at heart—one who can act his ass off too! Oh, and Hollywood, your boy is still here ready to kill it. See you soon.

12

TIMING IS EVERYTHING

"ADORE"

Song by Prince

You haven't heard much about the details of my sordid love life or relationships up until this point. I'm not claiming to have been a choirboy now; my bachelor days were definitely rock 'n' roll status. Many moments were completely unexpected and a little lawless. My stardom put me at the frontlines of the dating meat market of the 1990s.

Being a single, famous Black personality in Hollywood came with its privileges—trust me, there were plenty of perks! A real man will never kiss and tell, but I will confirm that my life certainly played out like a movie. As you're ascending into the stratosphere of fame, women are like stars in a clear night sky because they suddenly appear everywhere. Twinkling, flashing, and jockeying to see who can outshine the next. It was not the time or place for me to settle down at that point in my life. I was married to my dream. Many of my relationships were long-distance and not for any other purpose than to have fun. It was a situation of convenience mostly. I did not plan for a serious relationship; I was dedicated to my work and all its new opportunities. As far as I knew it, that was enough. Isn't it funny how we all like to think we've got our life completely planned out? I did; you couldn't tell me shit! Oh, you foolish young boy! Little did I know, love and fate have a funny way of changing your flight plans without asking for permission. As we know, God has a fantastic sense of humor.

Fate would have its way in my life. It would show me I'm not in control and that God's plan is far better than anything I could do for myself. Let me tell you how true love found its way, and how I met the love of my life, Kristen Baker Bellamy.

* * *

Love is no laughing matter, or at least true love isn't. There's that love that fuels your loins. Yeah, you heard me, the type of feeling that is just powered by the physical attraction that two people have between each other. A nice booty, a cute face, killer curves with a jacked-up personality. All that falls under this category. This type of "love" can fizzle and burn very quickly. It's fun, but it usually doesn't fulfill the fundamentals. Then there's deep, soul-gripping, *The Notebook*–type of love. It is gifted to you by the universe, giving you a new purpose and direction. This type of love grabs a hold of your heart, disables your normal functioning, and just won't let go. It makes you start to feel weird aches and pains in all sorts of places you never knew. That love takes you to places emotionally, both good and bad, that you never thought you'd visit. Nothing falls under normal operating procedures after that happens. Deep love is anything but normal. It's magic!

We all need love and want to be loved as human beings. No matter how fast you're rolling, or how popular and in demand you are, everyone at some point longs for true companionship from another person. The feeling is inescapable because it's a part of being human. It nags and claws at you in the quiet hours and minutes of your day. It taunts you when you're surrounded by a room full of adoring fans. It whispers to you after you've just crushed it at a performance. Loneliness plays cruel jokes. Just when your mind is telling you that you should be feeling as high as a kite and on top of the world, then you stop and realize there's nobody to relive your successes with when you go home. It never leaves you no matter how hard you try, or what vices you pick up to mash it down. It's still there, front and center. Some people stop and pay attention, others choose to keep on trucking, trying to bulldoze over and around it year after year. I've done both, but there came a time when love won. It fell out of a tree and hit me on the head. Bop! Just like a coconut! Here's how it all went down . . .

I was firing on all cylinders in my career. In the crazy world of show business, the entertainer ends up being the show. We often find ourselves moving too fast to even receive a blessing. If we're not careful, we can live our lives like a bullet train barreling through every station, every year, every milestone, with no pauses. One minute you're on a private jet flying out of one city, then you hop off and find yourself in the heart of another. I was surrounded by women everywhere I turned who exuded physical perfection. The crazy mind-blowing truth is that they would have all gotten down if I gave a simple head nod in their direction. Some of these chicks out here don't even have to know your freaking name. They're just attracted to the allure of fame. Fame is a drug. It can pull you in and destroy you if you're not mindful, because it's sexy and magnetic. It attracts some women toward you like a moth to a damn flame.

Many cats are gassed up by the attention and lure of having beautiful arm candy. Even if the candy makes her intentions well known that she's only sweet on you for what she can get. It's purely transactional. Fame by osmosis I call it! That's the sickness Hollywood has always suffered from. We're unconsciously grinding and grinding to reach a level of success where we can look back and feel like all the effort and sacrifice was worth it. That's how I was feeling in the building phase of my career. I was just like, Yo, I gotta get on, I gotta get on. They've got to know my name; I want to make it to the top. I want to succeed. Thoughts of settling down and having a family of my own weren't on my radar. Not one bit! To be honest, I didn't even know if it was for me at all.

Dudes don't usually have that same loud-ass biological clock ticking in their subconscious messing with their minds like women do. We won the genetic lottery in that department. I mean I felt like I was married to the game for a big part of my career. I was married to the never-ending, unpredictable grind associated with becoming famous for my craft. I had been at it for so long; it's all I knew. Fueled by that promise to never live in poverty, the promise I tearfully made as a teenager in the back of our family car, I poured everything I had into guaranteeing my success. I was married to making lots of money and traveling around the world, making my dreams come true. That's where my commitment was.

I was a star over at MTV, not just on my own program

Mom and Dad after moving to
New Jersey from the South.

A star is born.
Me at about six years old.

Love and happiness.

Rutgers crew! *(Left to right)* Bob Sumner, me, Martin Moore, Dewayne Dixon, Jacques Lucien, and Ron Workman.

Finding love in Miami with my soul mate, Kristen, while I was shooting *Any Given Sunday*.

Hollywood, I'm here! (1998)

Love of my life.

Photo by Bill Hayden.

Dance like no one's watching.

Photo by Bill Hayden.

Bailey on the way.
Photo by Brie Childers.

New beginnings! Fatherhood put me
on the path to my new journey.

Big Diesel and little B.

Three generations of Bellamy. *(Left to right)* Baron, me, and my dad.

Best day ever. Summers are made for grandparents.

Me and my sister, Karen.

Best of times with Julius.

First headshot.
Photo by Harold M. Maynor Jr.

The sacrifice has always been worth the results. My kids have become wonderful young adults. *Photo by Deborah Anderson.*

Shemar Moore.
Friends who are family.

Superstar Eddie Murphy on the set of *MTV Jams Live* with executive producers
Penny McDonald and Tracey Jordan.

Dad makes it to Hollywood! On the set of *Fast Lane*.

Me, Allen Iverson, and Chris Tucker at the Soul Train Awards.

Behind the scenes at *MTV Beach House* with Ananda Lewis.

Set life. Mom and Dad visit me on the set of *Fast Lane* with Peter Facinelli.

Life on the set of
Any Given Sunday with
Hall of Famer Terrell Owens.

On the set of *How to Be a Player* with my producing partners
Russell Simmons and Donna Chavos.

It's a Doggie Dog world.

RIP to my man Heavy D.

Chillin' with the one and only Ice Cube.

MTV Jams Live with Jodeci.

One in a million!

Mr. Late Night, Arsenio Hall.

Cool nights with Sam.

MTV Beach House:
The Hamptons with Tupac.

Brothers in comedy.
With Martin Lawrence.

The DPG (Dog Pound Gangsters) in
the house. *(Left to right)* Nate Dog,
me, Daz Dillinger, and Warren G.

One of the coolest chicks in the game. Me with Alyssa Milano.

Hanging with the legend of Nas!

Sign your name . . .
Me and Terence Trent
Darby.

Any Given Sunday with
Jamie Foxx. Miami, Florida,
1998 in South Beach.

either. I was unofficially the face of the entire network. I was cross-promoting my unique relaxed and relatable style of VJing, or hosting, on all the other shows: *TRL*, *MTV Top 40 Countdown*, *MTV Beach House*, *MTV Spring Break*, and *MTV Jams*. It was crazy.

I was even dabbling on the side in the music video scene, making appearances for artists like Tupac, Da Brat, Foxy Brown, Dru Hill, and others who had become my close friends. Then movies came calling like *Who's the Man*, *Love Jones*, *How to Be a Player*, and *The Brothers*. At that point, I had gotten this huge opportunity to play a part in this Oliver Stone football drama called *Any Given Sunday*. It was 1998 and I was already in the mindset of figuring out my next move in terms of stepping up my game professionally. This journey of self-discovery was as much about stacking my bank account as it was about leaning into my abilities as an entertainer with no boundaries. Who knew what I could do? Look at how much I was already able to achieve in such a short space of time.

I was fully invested in finding the answer to that question when the Oliver Stone project was presented. It was big-budget as I stated before. We're talking Al Pacino in *Scarface* big! Tom Cruise in *Born on the Fourth of July* big! As humbling as this opportunity was, I was anxious because I knew this could be my pathway to a whole other stratosphere of success in Hollywood. Professionally this was my shot to rack up a huge win! The self-inflicted pressure was on.

The film was slated to star Al Pacino, Cameron Diaz, Dennis Quaid, Jamie Foxx, James Woods, Matthew Modine, and LL Cool J. The way I saw it, this was a fascinating mix of Hollywood veterans and some of my contemporaries whose film careers were also on the rise. Storyline-wise, it was a win for me as well. It was a dude's type of movie, my type of movie. It explored the back-end life of those in the world of professional football. Players, coaches, agents, owners—everyone involved with bringing the life of the NFL to the masses on any given Sunday. Chronicling the lives of fictional star athletes in a very real way, it was showing the ups, downs, and gritty underbelly of playing football at the highest level. It was a story of sacrifice, loss, and triumph. All of which I knew far too well in my own life's struggles. It was perfect and I was perfect for it.

To show you how focused on crushing the role I was, I immediately went into student mode. I realized that I knew some things about acting, but I wanted to bring my A-game and seriously learn the craft behind it. I needed some in-depth insight into techniques that would transform a good performance into a memorable and great one. I was ready to crush it, so I found an acting class and signed up. I even took my skinny ass to the gym to bulk up a bit for the role. Oh yeah, I was serious as hell about it.

This dude named Greg Edelstein was the instructor of our class. This man was old school in his teaching and kept everyone emotionally accountable in his class. You had to dig deep and bring your truth in your acting on his stage. It was everything I needed. He was a very serious and strict methodical type of actor. Having perfect execution of your scenes was his sticking point. He was legit. As much as I was buying into his methods, I was also me and a true clown at heart.

Along with the other student actors in the class, we had an auditor appointed to observe our group. The role of the auditor was to observe the class and how the students reacted to the teacher. They were there to be somewhat of a teacher's aide. The name of our auditor was this girl named Kristen Baker.

I was in the class for a total of two or three months and entering my final few weeks before I had to leave to shoot the movie. One day Kristen came into class and sat down in the seat right in front of me. Sitting behind her I decided to crack open my pack of M&Ms and eat them. Your boy was h-u-n-g-r-y like a mo-fo! There I was gripping both sides of the bag and slowly, slowly trying to pry them apart without having the bag crackle and rustle too much. Good luck with that one! Instantly Kristen whipped around in her seat glaring at me and hissed, "You're being loud!" in a slightly annoyed voice. I sheepishly put the bag away and thought to myself, Who does this chick think she is? Little did I know, that would be the first of many times this woman checked my ass.

A few days later, we were running scenes and she joined the class late. There was nowhere else to sit so she sat right next to me. When she did, I turned to her nonchalantly with a nod of my head and said, "Hey, how are you doing?"

She turned to face me, "I'm good, thanks," she responded just as cool. Then she went on in a nervous jittery tone, "Oh my God, I know your girlfriend." Out of nowhere, just like that, but I was intrigued.

I was like, "Okay . . . I mean yeah, whatever. I know she knows a bunch of people."

"Yeah, I know her from modeling and stuff, and she talks about you all the time," she continued.

I must admit, I had no idea where the conversation was going, and it completely caught me off guard. I was dating this other girl named Julieanne Mijares at the time, and she was a super cool and connected fashion stylist. Julie knew everybody in the business because she styled video shoots for artists like Usher, TLC, and Dru Hill. Then Kristen curiously asked me, "Are you going to be gone for a long time with this new movie?"

"I know it's like a three- or four-month shooting schedule, so I don't know when I'm gonna see you next. It's a huge studio movie and kind of a big break for me," I answered because I really didn't know if I would be back in time to continue with any more of the class. Before you knew it, a few days later, she asked me to perform a scene with her. The scene was from a play called *Cheaters* of all things! The part we chose was about a couple who comes back from a wedding, and the girl is upset because now she wants to get married and the guy doesn't want to. Shiiiiiiiiit! I thought to myself. I already know this scene because I'm living this life! I don't even have to act. It just so happened that the girl I was dating at the time was dropping hints that she wanted to get married. The problem was that I was on a whole other wavelength and nowhere near a wedding chapel in my mind. I was laser-focused on heading out to kill it in this Oliver Stone movie. After I knocked it out of the park, I'd see what else was on the horizon for acting gigs. Plain and simple. I was pumped, ready, and focused—and my focus was definitely not on walking down no aisle any time soon. That's for sure!

A few days later Kristen and I began rehearsing for the upcoming scene at her apartment because we were scheduled for the next day. As we were acting out the scene, we got to a part where we had to kiss. Instantly I thought, Oh no, this could get really, really awkward. We never talked about it beforehand so I had no idea what she was thinking or how she felt about it. If I was going to actually kiss her, I decided to save it for when we were performing in class. This way it would be more spontaneous and real. I didn't even want her to know it was going to happen. I just wanted it to happen. So much for my plans. Before I even knew what was happening, Kristen's fast-ass leaned in and kissed me first!

On my mother, as soon as Kristen kissed me, my cell phone rang, and it was my girlfriend, Julie, calling. My mind was exploding. It was like she had put a LoJack on my goddamn lips! I reluctantly wrenched myself away, now dazed and a little confused, and I answered the phone. After a few quick replies and a nervous shuffling back and forth of my feet, I hung up. To this day I still can't tell you what the hell I said, but whatever it was, I was sweating through it.

The next day, our scene was a big hit. And, as the scene called for, we shared another steamy kiss. Damn, maybe I was better at this acting stuff than I even realized. I can't front, there was a little something there between us, but I wasn't quite sure what was happening. Our other classmates knew what was brewing before we did, they felt the chemistry too. The entire class made slick little comments like, "Ooh, y'all look so good together. What happened between the two of you? Did something happen? You guys are cute as a couple!" Third-grade playground shit, but I was secretly listening to it all and smiling to myself inside.

Off I went to Miami to shoot the movie. Hell, I basically moved there for it. Business as usual, right? Nothing but movie stuff only, right? Ah, no! I found myself calling Kristen back in Los Angeles on the regular to get "updates" on how the class was going. Everybody in the acting class was extremely high maintenance and going through varying degrees of life traumas. There was just all kinds of dramatic shit going on over there. It was like therapy, a comedy show, and a telenovela all rolled into one. It was ridiculous. Even though I knew the class was full of a cast of wild characters, I found myself looking forward to checking in and getting updates from Kristen. She would constantly call me as well. We'd laugh, make jokes, and talk for hours about anything. I looked forward to our weekly, sometimes daily, chats. One day I caught myself thinking, Shit, this girl has really gotten under my skin! It was like a light bulb went on and it got my mind churning.

With this realization, I decided to be a bit more intentional and to start with the tickets I'd gotten to the upcoming Super Bowl weekend in Miami. It was one of the rare weekends I wasn't scheduled to work. My first thought was to see if Kristen might be interested in flying down to hang out for the weekend. I wanted to see if I was just imagining our rising chemistry, or did she feel the same way? When I extended the offer to her, I also mentioned that she could bring a girlfriend with her as well to hang out. I wanted her to feel more at ease with the invitation and not weirded out by it. Hey, it worked, she took me up on my offer and our plans were set.

Just like a cruel joke, wouldn't you know it, I sprained my damn ankle during filming and was hobbling around the whole time Kristen was there. The crazy thing is that she wasn't pissed off or negative at all. She jumped right in and took care of me. This girl was so sweet, attentive, and nurturing. She made me start to feel certain things and get all nervous like I was a little schoolboy. What the Voodoo Priestess was going on up in here? Her friend eventually left Miami and Kristen ended up staying for the whole week. Just me, my busted-ass ankle, and her. I said to myself, Look at God. Look at God!

Weeks later when I came back to Los Angeles for Christmas break, I made a date with Kristen. We went to dinner at a swanky Latin spot called El Floridita because it was known for its great food and amazing salsa dancers. Low lighting, candles, a live band, and tequila. What a perfect combination! I had no clue what to order on that menu. When the waitress asked what I wanted, my ignorant behind answered, "Anything with chicken!" You know Black people and our chicken. Kristen stepped in and playfully guided me through, expertly introducing me to the wonderful world of Mexican food. We had a perfect official first date. Topping it all off, we finished up the night sitting in my car listening to the new Lauryn Hill album. As we sat there talking and laughing, the sexy duet featuring D'Angelo—"Nothing Even Matters"—came on. Like a scene from the movie *Love Jones*, a soundtrack of this moment, I can still remember the light cascading on her face. Her lips were so supple. I had to kiss them, and I did. A kiss that lasted for what seemed like an eternity! So dreamy and intoxicating I can still hear Lauryn's voice taunting, "Nothing really matters to me. . . " What can I say, I was clearly sprung.

Kristen was easy to be around, and we genuinely had the best time together. Undeniably we were drawn to each other for whatever reason. But, in true self-proclaimed bachelor form, I told myself that I wasn't looking for anything too serious at that point. So, she was the "homie." I had even met parts of her family on the first date that weekend in LA. During our dinner date, her best friend also unexpectedly gave birth. In the middle of dinner, she turned to me nonchalantly and said, "I don't know if you want to come to the hospital, but I gotta go see my girl. She just had a baby boy!"

I was like, "Fuck it. Let's go," and we went to the hospital in Pasadena. Now, remember, babies, family, settling down, and kids were the furthest things from my mind at that time, but here I was having a personal bedside visit at the hospital. I ended up meeting her sister, some more of her friends, and the whole nine yards. They were a cool bunch of people. She came from a genuinely nice family. Kristen was a good girl, "real people" as they say. I still wasn't too sure what we were doing, or how she felt about me. All I knew was the vibe was intriguing; sometimes in life, you just have to trust the experience.

We ended up sharing a weekend of exploration together. Touching elements from every angle in a seventy-two-hour period. It was like a condensed version of all things Kristen. Her love of music, family, adventure, and responsibility. Solid components that make up a real person. Wow! I had a great weekend with this girl, and it stuck to my bones like a good satisfying meal. I knew I had to return to Miami but my impression of her and what we shared was the beginning of something special. Truthfully, I still didn't know what this would mean in the context of my life, but I knew I had to explore all its possibilities. I was a bit hesitant and conflicted because I promised myself I'd remain hyper-focused on filming the movie. Opportunities this big didn't come around too often. We'd developed an amazing rapport and friendship that caught me off guard. Lacking any other solutions, I decided not to question things too much and just let the wave develop. This spark was something different I couldn't quite put my finger on, but somehow I intrinsically knew it was not a mistake. I would leave soon thereafter with a snapshot of things to come.

We would continue to communicate by phone regularly, not really tipping the scales but at a meticulous pace. When I think back now, I never really got a concrete diagnosis of how she felt about our weekend date. I had no idea whether she was looking for something serious herself. Fate would play a comedic part in this new romantic dance. It was like a coy game of love chess, where everyone was protecting their queen so to speak.

The truth of where we stood with each other was revealed in the funniest of ways. I called Kristen while she was visiting with her mom. When her mom answered the phone, she asked, "Who's calling?"

"Bill," I said a little apprehensively, feeling like I was back in high school.

"Ooh! You must be the guy my daughter won't stop talking about!" With that simple, familiar recognition, Mamma spilled the beans and gave up the goods on her daughter. Quickly after, I heard Kristen's horrified scream in the background, "Mom!" I was cracking up to myself. I could tell Kristen was mortified when she finally took the phone! It was like Ma had thrown a grenade right into the living room. B-O-O-M! BANG! Just like that, there was no going back for us. The truth was put on blast and somehow my decision had been made for me. Like third graders on the playground, we secretly fell deeply for each other; not just as friends either. Thanks, Ma!

That Christmas I made plans to come back to California to spend it with Kristen and her family. It was actually her mom and stepdad that I ended up spending time with. When I say these people did Christmas, I mean they did white picket fence Christmas! Listen, I grew up in the hood and we barely had room to create space for a nine-foot Christmas tree. We definitely ain't never had no real live tree! They had a real goddamn tree in their house and I was like, Oh shit! This must be the Brady Bunch!

To give you some background, Kristen is mixed so her mom is white and her biological dad is Black. They were two young people who met in college, fell in love, and made two beautiful daughters, Kristen and Melissa. You had the Brady Bunch on one side and the Jeffersons on the other side. When she showed me pictures of her dad, I never would have put her mom and him together, but it worked until it didn't. Kristen's mom and stepdad were so welcoming, family-oriented, and absolutely lovely. I was truly blown away for real. That's when I realized Kristen wasn't just another chick, but a quality person. Someone who came from great people. She was a special lady and I had to analyze this from a different lens.

Kristen was one hundred percent a product of her parents. She was kind, sweet, and held old-school values. She had me thinking about some things I had never thought of before. I thought to myself, Yo, this girl could literally be the mother of my kids one day. Shit! Did I say that? Hell, I was thirty years old after all. Maybe I had to pay closer attention to this one. I thought I knew that I didn't want to get married, especially right now. But, on the other hand, I had been in the dating game so long and had seen just about everything! I wasn't going to let a quality person slip away from me. I figured I was mature enough to explore the possibilities with Kristen because I knew she was solid. At the end, I decided to just be really fly and respectful of this situation, continuing to have fun with her and see what happened because we had so much in common. Both of us liked to travel, loved clothes and old-school music—she was made for me. Kristen most definitely had a nigga shook!

I decided, I need to meet this lady's biological father. Mr. Bernard Baker lived in Cleveland. When I finally got to hang out with him, I understood where she got her swagger from. He was just like one of my uncles; he was crazy just like them. That whole Black side of her family was my favorite. I thought, Lord have mercy, I know all these people; they are familiar for sure. Oh my God! I felt so comfortable. It was then that I fell even deeper for her. I admit I didn't fully understand the Brady Bunch side yet, but I knew they were cool. I had never dated anybody that was mixed-race before. In my neighborhood when I was coming up, you were either straight up Black or Puerto Rican. Or, if you weren't, you were a mixture of both. I never grew up seeing Black and white people getting together and dating. Never mind having families. Interracial relationships back in those days, even in the early 1990s, weren't as commonplace as they are now. It was just a different time. Somehow her mamma and her daddy found a way to defy the odds and make it happen. I am grateful to them for it. That must have taken a hell of a lot of courage. In the end, love won.

Two years later, on June 16, 2001, Kristen and I got married in Santa Monica on the beach. I proposed to her at Geoffrey's in Malibu, and I will never forget how it went down. I wanted to do it by the beach because I've always loved the natural calm that water induced. I knew what time the sun was supposed to set that day, so I planned accordingly. In my heart of hearts, I wanted to ask this woman to marry me in a way that would be completely different. It was planned perfectly through the process of intentionally misleading clues. I think she felt it was coming but didn't know how or when it would happen. I had arranged for the perfect table at Geoffrey's, facing the ocean. I planned for everything to be revealed in stages. I asked them to bring out their finest bottle of champagne. NO RING. Next came the wine and cheese. NO RING. Then Kristen was presented with their most delicious dessert. Still, NO RING! This must have been torture for her when I think back. Lol, let's not forget, I'm a comedian to the core and we play too much!

I eventually excused myself to use the restroom but crept out to the valet and put her ring above the passenger visor. When I came back to the table and grabbed the check, she had a little edge to her because I could tell she had no clue where this amazing date was going.

We drove from the restaurant to the beach with an odd silence hanging between us in the car. You could feel the undeniable tension that had built up. She seemed very pensive and was probably at a loss, thinking she was being pranked in some strange way. I know my girl was probably thinking this was some weird masquerade. No, it wasn't. I just had a plan to keep her guessing right up to the last minute. I finally rolled the car to a stop, facing Zuma Beach in Malibu. I turned to face her and told her she had something in her eyelashes that was about to go into her eyes. My ruse was perfect because it got her to pull down the passenger sun visor and bam . . . the ring fell into her lap! Kristen instantly exploded into tears, crying, "Oh my God! Are you serious?" She would not stop crying. I literally saw her body trembling with excitement, probably mixed with a little relief. Somehow, I was able to get her out of the car, but she was having a hard time getting her legs steady enough to support her. It was such a tender and emotional moment for us both. I was finally in a place I never dreamed I could be in, and she was in a place of not believing it was really happening. As fate would have it, just as the sun was setting, I got on bended knee and asked her to marry me! Once again, love had won!

Two years after being married, we welcomed our beautiful daughter, Bailey Ivory-Rose, into the world in 2003. And in 2006, our young king, Baron, came into our lives, making our family complete.

If somebody would have told me this is how my life would

turn out, I would have lost that bet. Timing is everything. It was the timing of meeting a woman that I thought was dynamic and taking the time to become her friend first. This is what made it possible for me in my life. Generally, I believe your blessings will come to you when you're least resistant. When you have your focus on living and just remain open to all life's possibilities. It's kind of like floating in the water without trying to swim. Your blessings will just flow and float right to you, making you stop and say, "Damn!" As the saying goes, nothing meant for you ever passes you by. I believe that's the through-line in life, its real beauty. That's the true secret of God's promise. You can rush some things in your life, but real lasting things often can't be rushed. They need time to grow. You must always stay ready for your season, or your reason. I truly believe God's timing is the best; it's actually flawless!

Being famous and chasing your dreams can sometimes test the balance of marriage. Finally, I had something for myself. My family is my precious jewel. I had won the heart of a girl that I had longed for and needed at this point in my life. I was fully invested while simultaneously cultivating my acting career. Family for me was a personal haven from the game. I had created a support system that would help me in so many other ways I didn't even know I needed help in. My personal and professional growth was multiplied tenfold. The responsibility of it all made me have more purpose. I loved embracing this new chapter.

I've never wanted to share too much of my personal space with the public. It comes with too many land mines. Once you open that Pandora's box, it's often incredibly hard to close it off again. You no longer have anything private left that's just yours. As it is, being a successful comedian already required me to use personal experiences to develop stories that my fans enjoyed. I've bared my soul many times. If I let people into the inner sanctity of my family's life, I feared I'd no longer be living for myself. When you allow everybody else to put their two cents in, that's what inevitably happens; you relinquish control, and you begin to move differently. Inauthentically if you ask me. My gut tells me, Yo, I got to protect my family. I can't let the game steal my family from me like I've seen happen to so many people. I didn't get to this point, build up such security, for all that mess to happen. That's why I stay conscious and vigilant, moving cautiously when I can.

Twenty years have flown by, and the journey has been incredible. I can say that having my family has made me a better man. Marriage has asked things of me that I never knew I could give. It has brought my life so much joy and rich experiences. I know I made the right choice. Love will always win with us. I'd make the biggest bet on that one!

13

PRIORITIES

"FAMILY REUNION"

Song by the O'Jays

Being famous is a crazy thing. I always knew I wanted to be a star. That seemed cool! What I eventually learned is that I didn't want or need to be Michael Jackson, Britney Spears, or Prince "can't walk out of the house level of famous." I wanted to keep going to the movies with friends I grew up alongside without feeling self-conscious or boxed in by it. I didn't want to become a caricature of myself like you watch some of these other celebrities become. It's like they're wearing a clown suit and don't have an identity of their own anymore. I've always wanted to be myself.

I love what I have chosen to do in life. I love to make people laugh and I love to see people smile. I love being creative and putting out content that can fill people up, make them think, and represent my Black culture in the best light possible. I love challenging myself by taking on new roles that will allow me to grow and reach new creative and professional heights. Levels I could have only dreamed of when I started out on this Hollywood journey. I love my loyal fans for their support and encouragement throughout my career. They've grown with me also, as I keep crossing new milestones. I love the professional and personal friendships I have made along my journey. I enjoy the money that I've made doing what I love. It has afforded me a life with peace of mind and material riches, enabling me to enjoy a comfortable life. A life full of monetary opportunities to continually bless those around me when I could. I often take inventory of all these blessings that comedy, acting, and producing have given me. It keeps me humble and keeps me hungry for more.

I say all of this to let you know that despite the love that I have for my chosen career path, there's nothing that compares to the love that I have for my wife and kids. I'd walk through blazing fire and back again for them! I'd slay dragons, tear down buildings, fight niggas, and anything else to make sure that they were okay. I'd give away everything I've built. All the accolades, adoration, and material things.

Much like fame, fatherhood was something I've always wanted and craved. I wanted to become a dad under well-thought-out circumstances, when I was really ready to commit. I didn't want to be a baby daddy with twelve kids here, there, and everywhere. I didn't want to bring kids into the world with just anybody. No oopsies or baby mamma drama for me! I'm not professing there weren't times, in my younger days, that I didn't wipe my brow and bite my fingernails hoping that I had dodged a bullet or two. For the most part, I moved into my romantic life with purpose too. I wanted a healthy, functioning environment to hopefully raise healthy kids. I was allergic to the drama. I had experienced way too much of it growing up.

I became a father to my daughter, Bailey Ivory Rose, in August 2003. She was the most beautiful flower I had ever laid eyes on. It was one of the most special moments of my life and a dream come true. My career was one thing, but being a new dad was indescribable. Wise people say things happen when they're supposed to, when you least expect them. The unexpected heavy weight of responsibility and consuming feelings of love I immediately felt was confusing. I had a new intensely deep symbol of what love is and it now existed outside of myself and my career. Bailey's birth represented a completely new beginning for me in my life, for sure. For the first time, I was feeling huge guilt and an emotional pull to do fewer gigs away from home. I was torn between my old love and my new love, but not for long.

There would be many lessons that came with our new bundle of joy. Lessons of time and commitment were introduced in this new chapter of my life. The most important lesson I learned being a dad is that I could freely give unconditional love. To be selfless and to love in crazy ways I didn't realize I had in me. Before having kids, I experienced getting married which highlighted one aspect of selfless love. Having to compromise, especially when you may not agree, was mind-blowing to me. It also helped me to mature by leaps and bounds. It required listening to someone else. That's marriage—give and take.

However, with your children, there's another level of love which is interesting. Your kids don't have to earn your love. They get it as soon as they enter this world and are delivered into your arms. Hell, you're already a sucker from the womb.

Babies don't have to prove anything to get everything. Boom! You're hooked! You shower them with all your love without even a thought. That revelation allowed me to love Kristen on an even deeper level too. Once we had Bailey, I knew it was possible for me to be a real-life superhero. My daughter's birth helped me give life to my deepest ability to love. It became my ultimate superpower.

I was right in the middle of filming the hit series *Fastlane* on Fox. We put in twelve-to-fifteen-hour workdays. I was number two on the call sheet, top billing, which came with increased pressure to be a stellar example. Free time was scarce, and I had a lot on my plate trying to juggle my newfound priorities. I was stressing trying to figure out how to manage it all. New show and new dad, who could ask for more? Little did I know, the thing that I craved the most once Bailey arrived was the time to enjoy it all.

Bailey melted my heart. Effortlessly, she renewed my purpose and gave a new ideological meaning to the concept of how I spent my time. Instantly! I wanted to be an incredible dad and was ready for all its challenges. My next thought: What the fuck am I going to do? I don't know how to be no daddy! I gotta do some on-the-job training real quick. Shit just got serious! I knew how to be a player, but knew nothing about how to be a daddy!

I had to get my diaper bag together. I went from Gucci to Goofy in the blink of an eye. Back then, Gucci was not fucking with no daddy diaper bags. I had to carry those flowery bulky joints making me look corny as hell. It was not fly at all. The diaper bag looked like a big old purse. As Will Smith said, "Love makes you do crazy things!"

When you have a daughter, she becomes your princess and

you become her knight. I was going to groom my baby girl to be a respectful, incredibly talented, and bright female who was self-assured. She was going to know from the jump that she was a queen. To know that she was full of Black girl magic and could conquer the world and her dreams.

I always thought that three kids would be awesome, but I would soon find out that two were just fine!

Juggling fatherhood while pursuing a demanding film, TV, and standup career was daunting. Try adding an additional child into the mix. However, in 2006 here comes my son, Baron. Be careful what you pray for, as the saying goes. I now had two kids under five years old. OMG! Things just got crazier. Meanwhile, I was reading scripts, auditioning, and doing national comedy dates. All while taking one kid to daycare as much as possible and helping my wife with nursing my son at night. Just falling asleep was a lost art during these times. Autopilot kicked in and I just blazed through my days unconsciously. I would pray for the day to end before it even started. I had no idea what grinding was until I had these three people in my life to grind for. I was hyper-focused on just functioning.

Baron was a great gift from the gods because I've always wanted to have a son. When I found out we had one on the way, I cried like a baby. I felt like I hit the jackpot! I already had a precious daughter and now I was getting my prince. Someone else to carry on my legacy, my name. Funny enough, I had no desire to make him a junior. I wanted him to have his own unique name. To be his own man and be able to flourish outside of my shadow, my successes, and my failures. Before we had him, I used to smile longingly whenever I'd see other guys with their boys. I would say to myself, Man, I want to have a son so I could teach him how to fish, how to hoop, to throw a football. I wanted to have those male-bonding moments where I showed my boy how to tie a tie, put on his wave cap, or how to clean his sneakers so they stayed looking fresh—just little stuff like that. When I had Baron, it was my opportunity to father in a different way than I was fathered. Mine wasn't terrible growing up, but with each generation, it's our job to evolve.

When Bailey was about four and in preschool, Baron was one and discovered he had legs and could run his momma ragged! It was truly hectic at home because I was starting to take off again professionally. I was back traveling around the country, working at full tilt. I had hungry little mouths to feed, college tuition to save for, and I couldn't afford to turn down anything. That's when Kristen laid down the law with me. My wife finally told me, "You need to be around more. Not only to help out but to also not miss out on all the precious moments that happen daily. It's not enough to just hear about the milestones secondhand. You have to see them. You have to be there to feel them!" As much as she was crying out for physical and emotional support, she also knew me well enough to know that not being actively present would cost me more in the long run. All that I had prayed for my entire life, I had waiting at home. The decision had to be made on how to handle it.

I had seen the cliché storyline of artists, stars, and musicians all going down a rabbit hole of trying to come back after a pause. It's a tough choice to delay dreams for family, but it was a worthy sacrifice. Many of my contemporaries had enjoyed incredible success in their careers and failed miserably in their family life. Hollywood is a tough business. If you slow down and take time off, what happens if you can't get back rolling? What if another star takes your place? What if the phone stops ringing? These are all the calculations I had assessed alongside my decision to step back. It wasn't only women who faced these dilemmas, and it took on greater weight because I was the sole breadwinner for my family. We had gotten used to living a certain lifestyle of blessings, private schools, vacations, and other comforts. Were we ready to lose something to gain something?

I bet on my family like I had bet on myself a decade earlier. It was the only thing I had that was truly mine and it was the only thing I would give my life for. My wish was to give my children the human side of me and not the celebrity side. So, I turned down work that would take me away from home for too long. I would wait for jobs that would fit my new lifestyle. Did it affect my career? If I'm being completely honest, I'm sure it did. I was good though because the quality time I spent raising my kids could never be exchanged for any job. My kids saw me all the time and I got the chance to learn from them, and them from me. I was Mr. Daddy Day Care! Mr. Carpool! Mr. Birthday Party!

Now, as Mr. Tuesday Morning Pancake Man, I would always show up at Baron's daycare events. I was the only Black father in sight, and everybody knew who Baron's daddy was. It was hilarious. I would sit up there with all those white mommies gossiping among themselves about who did what to who, and whatever crazy mess was going on at their homes.

For the longest time, my kids didn't even know I was famous. I never told them what I did for a living. It may seem weird, but I decided to save the details of my work for a later time when they were a bit older. My kids used to always say, "Daddy, why do you have so many friends? Did they go to your school? Did they grow up with you?"

I would laugh and say, "Yes, yes, they did. Daddy has plenty of school friends just like you."

The first time Bailey knew something was going on she was about seven years old and we were in the mall shopping. People started following us around from store to store and she turned to me and said, "Daddy, people are staring at you." I tried to ignore the comment, but she was very perceptive and persistent. At that moment I realized the time was running out on my "secret daddy" life. This was the time I selfishly wanted to keep for myself before I let the world in. I would be signing autographs in front of my kids when we were out in public, and the questions wouldn't stop flowing once we made it into the car. "Daddy, what are you writing? Why do they know your full name?" It was hilarious. I would eventually have to discuss my star life with my kids. Discuss what it meant, and how it provided for their lifestyle. I wanted to frame it for them in a responsible way. I would explain how I would have to leave for work soon, but that I would make my way right back to them shortly.

Dynamics and time requirements would change as my kids got older. They also got much smarter and harder to fool too. Kristen and I tried desperately to keep them in that bubble for as long as we could. Their friends, and their friend's parents, also had big-ass mouths. Kind of like the time when your child first comes home and announces that so-and-so at school told them that Santa Claus or the Tooth Fairy wasn't real. They would say, "I think you are famous, Daddy!"

"No, not really," I would respond.

"Oh, no, Daddy! You are on TV and I saw you on YouTube!" Clark Kent was about to be fully exposed as Superman. A huge part of my life had been put on hold and not revealed because I wanted the kids to focus on me as a dad. When we finally shared the truth with them, I was able to still keep that balance and have the best of both worlds. Proudly, they had those tangible experiences with me showing up as a regular old dad for so long.

Today, my kids' lives are so different from mine at their age. How they receive information is completely different. They are listening to and streaming music, movies, and TV shows differently. Then there's the huge vortex of social media. The new frontier is so vast and detached from my era. There used to be so much more structure in music and life. It's my job to bridge the gap between my life and theirs with love, exposure, and perspective. All while maintaining a protective grip on their innocence.

Proudly, my love of music, fashion, and culture are in their DNA. They got it in a double dose because Kristen shares the same love as well. I can't decide whether I've had more teachable moments with them as teenagers or as youngsters. The young adult lessons have been different; they seemed more crucial to get across.

Parenting teens and young adult children is hard. I wanted to be that strong reminder of the hierarchy that exists no matter who you are. Everyone has to answer to somebody. I also wanted to be that cool, you can talk to me about anything sort of parent so I could guide them on a different level.

With a daughter and a son, I always tell people it's like AM/FM radio. Their frequencies are different; they don't receive or process information in the same way. As a father, I had to address them differently if I truly wanted to understand them. Communication with my kids has been like fiddling around with that old broken-down transistor radio your dad had in the garage. I had to adjust to find out what station my daughter was on. Then readjust in a different direction to find my son's station.

Once I figured out their call numbers, that's when I heard what they were transmitting. Only then could I listen to them and bridge the gap in helping to solve problems.

No matter how well you raise your kids or shower them with love, everything is not always sunshine and roses. Sometimes they don't get it and think they're too damn smart for their own good. We go back and forth about being scared if we're doing them a disservice by keeping them so comfortable and secure. Don't get me wrong, I would never ever put them in harm's way, but we also can't figure everything out for them either. It's a skill you have to hone as a functioning individual. Instability and a little bit of discomfort around your next move build a hell of a lot of character too. I owe my career success to this uncomfortable uncertainty, quite frankly. Yeah, they're great kids, but they're also not kids who know anything about the hood life I grew up in. It's both a blessing and a curse of overcoming poverty. I have celebrated the victories of my rise, but on the other side you sometimes end up overcorrecting with your kids.

I don't want to say no to my kids just to say no, but in some instances, you must. Just because you can is not the reason to give your kids everything they want. When I say no, I give them alternate ways to get to where they want to reach. I give them a challenge like, "If that's a goal you want to reach, you can do X, Y, and Z first. Then we'll talk about getting what you want." It's got to be about work, then reward. If there's no requirement on their part, that's how you create entitled brats. In the natural progression of life, at some point, they're going to have to earn their way, one way or another. To keep a roof over their own heads, or eventually keep food on their family's table, they will have to lead the way. And, if they don't have to worry about financially supporting themselves, they have to earn the respect of the people they interact with. Money can't always buy you everything!

In my book, Black children need to understand what adversity is. It's important to their DNA because adversity is America—it's our America. In our America, they're still trying to put up booby traps in broad daylight so we can't vote. Yeah, man, some of these white folks out here work overtime to guarantee we stay in our place—under their feet. They're not ready to deal with Black folks as equals. Not everyone is ready or happy to have a Black family going to their schools, walking in their neighborhoods, or eating at their restaurants. No matter what that Black family's net worth and social status. I've seen it firsthand; nobody can tell me differently! I need my Black kids to always be alert to the underlying current that moves the country and world they live in. The deeply rooted belief of separate, but not equal.

A few years back, I had to have a talk with my daughter about acting a little irresponsible with the car we got her. I got a little whiff of some entitled little "rich girl" shit starting to creep in and I had to shut it down immediately. I did not like what I was seeing. She may have gone to private schools, but I always reminded her that we are not "of" private schools. I come from the struggle of the streets, don't get it twisted. I know what's real and what's not. I said to her, "Bailey, you know I bought my first car myself, right? So, it meant something to me. It meant that I missed hanging out with my friends and buying nice things because I had a goal." She looked at me without a smile on her face, just staring and blinking her big brown eyes begging for me to get on with the lecture. I continued, "Now if you had to buy that car you have, make the payments, and get insurance, it would be a whole other get down to you. You wouldn't have people up in there acting the fool and disrespecting your property! You'd be like, Yo, yo! No, you are not smoking in my car stinking it up!" I've seen kids who'd trash their shit in a minute and not think twice about it. The reason being, they knew a newer and better version would be handed to them. Not me. Not in my house!

Just as much as your kids can fuck up, they can also make you so damn proud to be alive! Bailey did that for us recently. My baby got into an Ivy League college in the most remarkably ironic and memorable way.

My best friend from college, Martin, is still a huge part of my life. His daughter went to Princeton on a full-ride scholarship. That young lady is so freaking smart and an all-around wonderful person it would blow your mind. She was the first Black member of their family to go Ivy League. During the process of Bailey applying to colleges, I told my boy Martin, "Yo, my daughter's got to go to college and I have all the schools that we're waiting on replies from."

He said, "Yo, B man, Bailey's gonna go to Ivy League, man."

"That would be hot! That would be hot!" I said.

"I see it, B. She's smart. We're gonna be the only two dudes in the crew whose kids broke through into the Ivy League. I believe that!"

A few weeks later, I was shooting this movie *A Rich Christmas*, and Martin called me up out of the blue suggesting, "You know what you should do, B? You should write a letter to your daughter. This is what I did for mine. You should write a letter to Bailey now, speaking to her as if she already got into her first pick school. And, when she does get into that school, I want you to give her the letter. In it thank her for her commitment, congratulate her on her victory. Write it now from the mindset like it already happened."

That idea blew my fucking mind! I said, "Oh shit! Are you serious?"

He replied, "Do it right now while you're thinking about it. Put today's date on it too." So, I sat there in my trailer, before I went on set, and secretly wrote my baby girl a heartfelt full-page letter. And then I filed it away.

Fast forward a few months when all of her acceptance letters came in and I was wrapping up shooting on the movie. She got accepted to all these amazing schools but got waitlisted for the school she desperately wanted as her first choice. Kristen and I resigned ourselves to the fact that maybe she wasn't going to go Ivy League after all, but that would still be okay. Even the dean of admissions from her top school called us on Zoom and shared that he thought Bailey's application and portfolio looked amazing and incredibly strong. Unfortunately, he just didn't have a space to offer her at that time. She was disappointed for sure, but we told her that if she took an offer at one of the other great schools and she didn't like it, we wouldn't force her to stay there.

Wouldn't you know it, the same afternoon I came back home from shooting she got pulled off waitlist status and was officially accepted into the Ivy League school she had been dreaming of! That's how God moves! I came home and my wife and daughter were sitting there waiting for me grinning really hard with the university's sweatshirts on. When I realized what was really going on, I instantly became super emotional. I couldn't pull myself together, but my daughter didn't understand the full reason why I was so overcome. She thought I was just happy she finally got into her desired school. She didn't know that months earlier her daddy made that affirmation and lifted her desires up into God's hands. This was just confirmation and manifestation of the power of God working in my life, in my family's life! A validation that our hard work and sacrifices were not for nothing.

I went into my bedroom and got the letter I had written months prior. I was trembling when I laid it in her hands saying, "I believed in you before you believed in yourself!" I told her to open the letter and look at the date. Then I took the letter from her and read it out loud. Oh, my goodness! Your boy Bill Bellamy was a mess, but it felt beautiful. The letter was as much a gift to her as it was to me. The words flowed like I had written them that very day. There we all were, in our living room, crying our eyes out in such joy. I had my boy Martin to thank for this extra gift and for this unforgettable family moment.

That journey was not only a lesson for Bailey, it was a lesson for us all. A lesson to be focused, committed, and unwavering in pursuit of our biggest dreams. A lesson to never write them off when we encounter hurdles. Leap over those motherfuckers and keep pushing forward. Baron witnessed her drive and it will be a lesson he'll take with him forever. Not only does he have the stellar example of a strong and amazing mother, he sees the quality woman his sister is blossoming into. He sees Bailey's strength, her wisdom, and admires her for it. Eventually, when he spreads his own wings to fly, he will choose the women in his life with his mother and sister as a benchmark.

Life has taught me that you've got to have priorities. Having my family gave me my roots and the levity I needed to brave the storm of this journey. They truly gave me something to fight for. My children were a gift outside of the game, outside of the hustle. Their birth allowed the delivery of my greatest phase of manhood for me. Up until they were born, my whole focus was to make it in show business, be a huge star, make millions of dollars, and win an Oscar. Although those dreams still exist for me, I had to find the balance that I needed to do it all. Striking the balance to not only do it all but also be present and equally participating while doing it. Not just checking the boxes and going through the motions. To be the leading man on the big screen and in my personal life as a husband and dad.

One thing I think all actors who've had successful marriages have in common is that they see their job as a job. It has a clearly defined role in their lives. It's what they do. Everybody does something for a living. Once you leave your job, you have to know how to take off that hat and come home and be husband, wife, dad, or mom. You've got to be able to separate the two. To give the same priority to your home life as you would give to your job. I had to remember to stay grounded and tethered to this earth, as a celebrity, and not get caught up in being a star who's way out there.

I gained much more than I lost following through with my decision to put my family's needs first. I have my wife to thank for that. Being strong and faithful enough to make "us" work enabled her to alert me early to the fact that I was fucking up. I refocused on the real riches that I had accumulated, the real stuff that matters. Work is what I do, but I didn't make my life all about work anymore. For the first time in my life, I pumped my brakes.

Being a comedian is what I do, being an actor is what I do, being a philanthropist is what I do, but at my heart of heart, I'm a son, brother, husband, and dad. I'm just an inner-city kid from Newark, who dreamed bigger than life.

My life's goal is to continue to help change the narrative of how a Black man shows up in this society. To challenge the stereotypes about how he loves those around him. You invest in your family like a stock. The dividends are not always revealed in the first quarter; being a parent is a marathon, not a sprint. My advice to my fellow brothers would be to stay the course and do the work. The payoff is tremendous and the moments shared are priceless. Careers are incredible but family is irreplaceable.

14

SHOT CALLER: MY WAY

———

"MY PREROGATIVE"

Song by Bobby Brown

Good is not good enough when extraordinary is possible!

Your talent makes room for your calling. It makes a seat for you at the table where decisions and choices are being made. I firmly believe the life I have lived is a testament to this fact. There ain't no mistakes when you see your blessings and the fruits of your labor unfold before you. All you have to do is open your arms and gather them up; you must be mindful to openly receive the bounty and not retreat in fear.

Right now, with my kids old enough to fly on their own, I'm making my way back to the table. Actually, I'm making my own table and all the people that are worthy will be seated.

Recently one of my homeboys said some shit to me that fucking hit me really hard. He said, "Bill, why don't you accept being

193

the special star that you are? Why do you have to always revert to being so humble?" I was stunned into silence, and I rarely get stumped. He continued with his gut-punch insight, "Why do you feel like you've got to bring yourself down a notch, or be overly nice to folks because you want them to like you?" I still had no answer. I stayed silent. He continued, saying, "Listen, man, it's your turn right now to turn it up! Don't nobody want to be regular! Everybody aspires to be like a star, so you got to be the star that you want to inspire people to be."

"You know what? Damn, that's deep shit!" I finally replied.

He said, "Man, you got to turn your vibration all the way up. All the motherfucking way up, you hear me? That's gonna change everything. You got to turn it up. Stop catering to other people and stop focusing on being nice. Just be you!"

"Fuuuucck!" I replied.

"Because that's what's gonna make people want to be around you, to push for you because they want to have that energy you bring."

"Got it," I said, trying to process in real time all the truth he was preaching. It was so profound and deep and exactly what I didn't know I needed until he said it. It was pouring over me like medicine to my soul.

"Don't channel the common man's energy my friend. No-body wants to copy what they are doing themselves. You are special, so believe in that." His finishing words of wisdom stuck with me. Correction, they haunted me.

Those profoundly deep and personal insights came from a man who is like a brother to me. No, he's not a therapist, life coach, agent, or doctor; he's a real fucking friend. This guy's a true example of the type of strong brothers I surround my-self with. Brothers who have always been in my corner rooting for me in good times and in bad, in struggle and in prosperity. They've always remained steadfast and true, calling the balls and strikes along the way.

After the pep talk, I marinated for a few days in his words of wisdom. I didn't have much to say during our talk, but I mulled it over in my mind hundreds of times. His words had cut deep into my psyche and exposed my soul. Once I truly felt like I absorbed it all, I charted an inner course for myself. I said to myself, This is what I'm gonna do. I am going to turn my light all the way up. All the way up to the brightness levels like before I got married, before I had kids.

As part of my journey to making sure I was present to raise well-adjusted kids, I turned my light down to a flicker. I turned my shit down for my wife, for my kids, for everybody so that my fame didn't get in the way of me showing up as husband or as daddy. I made that choice willingly, and it was what I needed to do at the time.

Today, however, I resolve to myself, I'm not turning down my fire for anybody else no more! Y'all niggas gonna get on my page and come up to where I am! Up to where I vibrate or it's just not gonna happen! And, guess what? As soon as I made that mental switch, major shit started to shift in my life. I started to book major talk show appearances promoting my body of work, and you know I showed up fly as fuck! Just like old times, playa. I'm turning up on these motherfuckers! I promised myself they were going to see Bill Bellamy. They weren't going to say, "Oh yeah, that's just Bill." I wanted everybody to say, "Aww damn! My God, that's Bill Bellamy!" Then I want them to say to themselves, "Wow, he's still the same, but even better this time around!" That's the reaction I was going for.

* * *

Comedy will always be the heart and soul of my business and my brand. I've finally gotten to the place where I am condensing my time more efficiently. I'm doing fewer shows for more money. As far as my content, I've grown and have so much more real-life shit to talk about. Being married twenty years, raising motherfucking kids, the ups and the downs, middle age, and COVID-19! There are so many experiences to draw from and the contrast to my younger self is bonkers. I'm glad I was able to live long enough to be able to talk about all this shit we're going through. People always say to me, "Bill, you don't ever seem like you have no bad days. You're always motherfucking smiling and shit! You've always got good energy."

All I can do is look at them and smile back because that means I'm good at what I do. We all have struggles, but nobody is paying to see my comedy show just to leave there more depressed than when they arrived. My job as a comic is to make them laugh. To make them laugh so freaking hard they forget about their own shit. I want to make them think about the other shit that really matters. To educate and to inspire—that's the mark of a great comedian.

* * *

I started my production company Bill Bellamy Entertainment Inc. in 2005 and executive-produced small projects like the family-friendly comedy series *Who Got Jokes* for TV One and *Ladies Night Out* and *Crazy Sexy Dirty* comedy specials for Showtime, which were a little more risqué. Mostly, the company lay dormant for a while. With my newfound spark, I am working on producing multiple series to sell to a network. Shoot, the way distribution is now, my goal may be realized on a streaming platform. Netflix, Amazon, Hulu, HBO Max, Disney Plus, Apple TV—the sky's the limit.

I want to produce content that reflects the positive side of the Black experience. To show not only the struggles, hardships, and redemptive stories, but also the everyday regular Joe ones in our community. There are Black bank executives juggling busy careers, Black mothers doing PTA bake sales, being entrepreneurs and bosses. Black soccer dads who are also engineers, creators, and trailblazers in every sector. We have been here doing all these things even before TV gave us our props. Our stories matter and seeing us doing dynamic, normalized things provides a roadmap for generations to come—for my great-great-grandkids. I want my work going forward to be evergreen. That's the type of content I will create from here on out. Shining a spotlight on the levity that exists in our community is important to me.

Over the last decade, I've learned the truth about the success game in Hollywood, and it's not just about how many leading-man roles you rack up on your IMDB resume. I learned that the true power comes from producing your own projects and creating your own shit. From here on out, I will only do projects that I can also produce. When you have that credit on a project, you have more weight in the game. As an artist more creative power dictates how the narrative is told. It's about collecting that back-end money; that's what counts. Earlier on in my career, I got my check and was cool with it. I showed up and did as I was told. Then, I went home to wait on the next role to be offered to me. Waiting for the scraps like a trained lab rat. No more waiting for me.

Activating my promise to myself, one of my newer movies, Tressa Azarel Smallwood's *A Rich Christmas* which I produced for BET+, was a triumph because I played the leading-man role as well. I secured my girl Victoria Rowell, a talented actor and humanitarian, who stepped in and did a great job directing the film.

A switch for sure, because I got to showcase the responsible dad side of me, the Mr. Bellamy side. In it, I play this guy named Marshall Rich, product of the foster care system, who is incredibly cool and humble. He worked hard to make a successful life and at the age of twenty-four was able to buy the foster home he grew up in. Then he went on to build an impressive empire, purchasing hotels and commercial buildings in Washington, DC. In the midst of his rise to wealth, he got divorced, and Marshall got full custody of their daughter. Tapping into my fatherhood experience, I brought a warm and tender realness to the role that made me proud. When I first saw the story, I said to myself, I know how to be a dad, I can do this.

I put this young actress named Tyler Abron in the role of my spoiled bougie daughter, Valerie Rich, who eventually learns a valuable lesson in humility and gratitude through service. Actress Vanessa Estelle Williams plays my ex-wife (Aggie Maggy) and Denise Boutte plays my new romantic love interest, Lauryn Smith. It's a really cool story that shows the uncomfortable vulnerability and uncertainty men sometimes face when dating. You get to see me on the hot seat sweating it out. I love that Marshall was not a slick player dude. He's honest, successful, and full of integrity; I admire him as a character. It's a feel-good holiday love story that just happens to have a Black cast. Who can't connect with the principles of love and redemption? Those are the type of real projects I love; they have no color stamp on them.

Another new movie project I'm proud of is *Back on the Strip*. I got to costar alongside some of the funniest comedians in the game and it was wild. Wesley Snipes, Kevin Hart, Tiffany Haddish, Faizon Love, J. B. Smoove, and Gary Owen; this cast should've been fucking illegal. I have never laughed so much in my natural born life! It was like the perfect homecoming for me because we're all friends in real life.

The movie's about the crazy stripper antics and characters on the Las Vegas scene. Behind the camera, we were cracking jokes all day long! It wasn't like we were even working; more like we were hanging out. The funniest part came when we had to do our stripper routines. I didn't really realize how hard it was to be a stripper. Just two wiggles, a shimmy, and a pump pump; I thought that's all it took to act like a stripper. Coordinating the moves, doing it in front of folks, and then trying to look sexy and serious had me trippin'! I was up on stage all out of breath and shit trying to look good, feeling all awkward. No wonder strippers are in such great shape, they dance and practice all day long and consume nothing but a cardio diet. It's unbelievable how much conditioning and skill it takes. Yeah, that shit is hard! Hat's off to the strippers. I'm definitely not quitting my day job for all that.

If I want to be up in something, I'll stick to the social media game; it has me working overtime. I sure wish it was around when I was coming up. That shit would have saved me so much wear and tear on my body and car. My social media pages have become like my own private sound stage for comedy. It's fantastic because in between appearance and movie projects, I can stay in direct contact with my loyal fans. I love to reminisce, telling stories of personal behind-the-scenes antics that never made it into the headlines. I crack myself up thinking about the crazy shit I've seen and done, and the even crazier eccentric folks who've crossed my path. Writing this very book has inspired me to look back on my life and appreciate how far I have traveled to get here. It hasn't always been easy, but it has been authentically my path. Many cats go through life and never take the time to reflect on their choices. Reflecting allowed me to make the necessary adjustments to fine-tune my approach so that I could continue to grow.

I've also been throwing my hat into the podcast ring, with my *Top Billin'* spot, and it is doing remarkably well! Almost one year ago I launched the real talk platform and it has been one of the best professional moves I've made. Bringing together sports stars, comedy icons, musical superstars, and others I've admired from near and far, I've been able to create my own playground where anything can happen. It can get pretty damn wild when people know they're in a safe zone for sharing their thoughts. We laugh while having deep discussions about everything under the sun: kids, politics, work, other people. I often find my guests taking a trip down memory lane with me. They usually share what they learned about themselves, and others, through their struggle to the top. Reminiscing about the soundtrack to their own lives and what songs helped carry them through and get them over the bumps along the way. *Top Billin'* is my own grown-up damn treehouse and it's as natural to me as getting on a bike and peddling. When your goal is to make people have fun without the drama or stuffiness, it's amazing what you hear and how deeply you can connect. I'm proud of this venture and excited to see where it can ultimately lead.

Today I'm back! I'm firing on all cylinders, doing a ton of projects. I always say, "You have to be out there doing it because nobody knows you when you are in the lab thinking about it." You have to be visible and bold with your ideas.

God's timing is always flawless to me and it's amazing. When God decides that it's your season there's nothing or nobody that can stand in your way. You've always got to ride your wave and continue to plant your seeds because you don't know when they're going to bloom. So, I'm just putting my head down and doing the work with conviction right now. Making a hole and dropping one tiny seed in at a time, covering it up, watering it, and then moving on to plant the next one. The sun may be beating me down like a motherfucker sometimes, but it's also necessary to reap my harvest later on.

As far as being an actor or producer it's a different game today. The networks are suffering and they're thirsty for good content. We have never had so many opportunities to place content with so many outlets. It's a plus, plus, plus landscape. No more being at the mercy of a few big networks who were once dictating to creators what they're buying or what viewers want to see. Shit, truth be told, creators never even saw themselves in such a powerful light; we always had the mindset that we were coming to the table hat in hand begging for a shot. Now, we accept the offers and consider the platform before we turn over our intellectual property. In many ways, the table has shifted and we are more equal partners. We're the Napster now. We hold the power to the stories of the people and there's a streaming service for everyone. This is the Y2K boom and bust for the movie and television industry. Everything's up for grabs.

What's my wish for Bill Bellamy 2.0? My greatest wish is that he steps into his light fully expecting to slay and conquer. No limitations, no regrets, and no brakes!

15

MAKING IT THROUGH

"DREAMS AND NIGHTMARES"

Song by Meek Mill

Recognizing the amazing value that life holds means coming to the realization that you must let some shit go. It allows me to live my life to the fullest, always mindful that nobody knows what tomorrow promises. I've had to learn how to forgive a lot of people for different things because I couldn't keep holding on to goofball shit. Working through and moving beyond hurtful past stuff allowed me to continue to grow. I finally figured out that holding on to anger or grudges depleted me more than it affected those who did me wrong. Grudges are toxic and will eat away at you like cancer consuming everything and everyone you care about.

People will take you for granted; that's a fact you can bank on! I think one of the hardest things that I've learned in my career, and in my life, is that love is not guaranteed to be reciprocal. Effort is not always received as effort or returned in-kind. I had to learn to love someone else in the same way I wanted to be loved back. Regardless if it came back to me with the same purity or not. Giving out the energy that I wanted to receive is an act of self-love I indulge in. You just have to accept that whatever comes back is beyond your control. Don't withhold kindness either because you feel like you've been wronged or burned. Give it out. I decided long ago to let it authentically be a part of who I was. It's good for my soul to let that energy come out. I don't let other people dictate my attitude or the intensity of my actions. If you want to be a loving person, be a loving person. You might love all the wrong people in the process, but at least you'll know you have the ability to give love. Claim that as a win because not everybody can say that.

To some folks, at times comedians may seem like they are superheroes. Often invincible and damn near impenetrable, or immune to thoughts of negativity and sadness. The reality is that there's a dark side to comedy and funny niggas crack too.

Comedians' sole purpose is to get a laugh out of people they don't know. Often, we do it at the expense of our own feelings or mental state. Even if we're in the middle of having a shitty life situation, we still step on stage dead set on making someone else forget their worries. Your audience pays to be entertained, and that's all that matters. When you think about the reality of that, it seems either messed up or completely self-destructive. You only have to look at Richard Pryor, John Belushi, and one of my idols Robin Williams to see prime examples of the darkness that can coexist with people in our line of work. Making people laugh for a living doesn't make you immune to your personal pain. Making others feel good does not mean that you feel good within yourself. Having to consciously exist in that gap between reality and perception is most likely a contributing factor in funny men and women getting to a destructive place and sometimes going over the edge.

* * *

Sometimes the only thing you can do is put one foot in front of the other and just put up enough fight to make it through to see another day. There've been days when the ability to press forward was my biggest win and my best accomplishment.

To say that life can be difficult is a major understatement. It was difficult for me professionally for a number of reasons. Breaking through in the comedy world was brutal. It was sometimes difficult overcoming color barriers, difficult crossing over to the next level in Hollywood. All of these difficulties didn't compare to the utterly life-shattering moment I experienced the loss of my only brother, Julius, and the loss of my mother shortly after. Difficult doesn't even begin to describe those years of painful darkness.

In 2014 I lost my brother, Julius; he was only thirty-two years young. It is fucked up and there's no other way to put it. He was way, way too young to leave this earth, and selfishly I wasn't ready for him to be gone from my life either. My brother was severely overweight and a Type 2 diabetic who sadly never took his condition seriously.

Julius loved sweets more than he loved living, it appeared. I know it sounds cold to say it like that, but that's the cold truth. My brother ate sweets morning, noon, and night. He even opened his own damn bakery making cookies, cakes, and other super unhealthy shit like that. As you can imagine, not only did he make all that stuff to sell, but he also taste-tested everything he made. This was the wrong damn business for someone with his condition, especially for someone with such a lack of self-control. Sweets were an addiction for Julius and it broke my heart every time I heard him get excited about stuff he was cooking up. I did everything I could to help him change his lifestyle or take his condition in hand. Every suggestion, every recommendation, introduced him to people who could help him; but he, unfortunately, chose differently.

When he decided to open his bakery, I remember saying to him, "Julius, bro, you can't eat that shit every damn day, man!"

"Well, I gotta taste it! Mommy's gotta taste it, Daddy's gotta taste it. I made the shit. This is what I do," he would reply defensively.

I let the issue slide because I was proud of him for starting his own business and doing his own thing, but it bothered me at the same time. I wanted to see him happy and successful. It couldn't have been easy for him to grow up in my shadow and be the youngest child. I know that, this is why I had such a soft spot for Julius. He was my baby brother and damn near could have been my son because of our age gap.

On the day that Julius died, he wasn't feeling well all day because apparently his insulin levels were low. To compensate for his imbalance, we later learned that he had drunk an entire sixty-four-ounce soda. I don't know if you can visualize sixty-four ounces, or know how much sugar is in one can of soda, but just imagine that multiplied by almost five and a half times. That's what he drank in one sitting. That sixty-four-ounce shit was always pushed really hard at fast-food spots in certain neighborhoods. Then people wonder why a bunch of Black folks have diabetes. It's baked into the master plan. After drinking that big-ass soda my brother went into what they call diabetic shock. They listed his cause of death as being morbid obesity. Remember, like I mentioned before, he was just thirty-two.

To this day, I don't drink soda.

Two years later, in 2016, I lost my mom and it was just too much for me to bear. Edna was strong-willed right to the very damn end. As I got older, and she got sicker, it drove me crazy. You could never win an argument with her and she was always right, just like when I was a kid. My mom also suffered from Type 2 diabetes. She had a stroke, bounced back from the stroke, then had a massive heart attack not too long after that. That was how it ended for her, that's what ended up taking her out of this world. All of this happened within the span of three years.

It was crazy and felt like I was living day after day in my worst nightmare. I clearly recalled saying to myself, I don't think I'll get out of this thing. All of the pain was just too deep and unrelenting and I felt like I could find no peace. There was no place I could go and nobody that could soothe my hurt. I was lost in my own sorrow and found myself drowning.

After my mom had been diagnosed with diabetes and had her stroke, the doctors wanted to put her on medication, but she refused. Her stubbornness was maddening and once she got something into her head you could not budge that lady. Not even an inch. Mom would say, "I'm not taking no medication because I worked for a pharmaceutical company and I know about side effects." She wasn't wrong about side effects, but it was about weighing the pros and the cons, and she was not open to that grey area. It was either black or white to Edna. She would do a little research and say, "If I take these diabetes pills it will mess with my heart and my kidneys. I don't have anything wrong with my kidneys now but this medication could mess them up. Then, the doctors will put me on more drugs to control my kidneys, so I'm not going to take that pill. I'll be alright."

It got to the point where my mom had to go to the bathroom every two minutes and her vision started to get worse. She still managed to see well enough to sit around all day long shit-talking and slinging her verbal daggers at everyone. She was a trip! As infuriating as she could be, my mother was still cracking me up with her sharp humor until the end.

Her diabetes started to get progressively out of control because it wasn't being treated. One day I broke down and had a heart-to-heart discussion with her, pleading, "Mom, you are walking down a perilous pathway and you've chosen to take the entire family on this crazy reckless ride with you. I just need you to fully understand that your neglect for yourself is going to affect other people."

"I don't care. It's my life. You can live your life, I'm gonna live mine. I'm not worried about a stroke!" That's what she would say to me when I tried to reason with her. There was that defiant warrior I always knew growing up!

The choice was made. She didn't want any medications and we couldn't force her to care about getting the help she needed. My mother was too smart for her own damn good. Even though she had actual medical knowledge, she refused to use it to her advantage. She took the pessimistic route with it. Instead, she used her pharmaceutical insights to sabotage herself and rob us of having her in our lives longer. I wonder if seeing Julius die well before his time caused her to give up on her own life?

Her memorial service was on July 14 and it was memorable for many reasons. One of which was the way I heard my dad speak about Mom in his speech. It really blew my mind and opened up an entire uncharted section within my soul.

In my entire life, I never heard my dad say that he loved my mom. I always assumed he had loved her. My parents had been together for so long and been through so much, but I never heard him say the actual words: "I love you, Edna." I never heard him say the words to me or my siblings, Karen and Julius, either. When he said, "I love you, Edna" at the memorial, it struck me harder than I thought because the words were so simple yet so profound.

All my life, in the absence of those three simple words, I had unconsciously filled in the blanks. In doing so, I absolved my dad from his humanistic responsibilities to his family and to the woman to whom he pledged his life. As his son, I should have heard him use those words to my mother daily when she was alive to hear them herself. I wonder if some of the tears my father shed that day were because he realized the very same thing. I wonder if he recognized that he had selfishly withheld his love and it cost him more than he had realized. The void was revealed at mom's memorial; revealed for all of us to see. Maybe all these years he himself didn't realize his omission. My dad stood in front of everyone that day looking like a heartbroken, defeated, and lost man. This vision of him took me over the top.

My father had written my mother a letter and read it out loud. That may not seem special to most people, but for me, I never knew my dad could write such a heartfelt speech. I had never seen him write on a piece of paper before. Now, there he was standing in front of everyone pouring his heart out on three handwritten sheets. It was unbelievably gut-wrenching, and such a revelation to me. It dawned on me during that moment: I never knew my dad as this kind of man because he never revealed that side of himself to us. He lived most of his life never expressing love or his truest feelings, as if it was taboo or something. I never realized how much I needed to hear those words expressed by him. It hit me like a bullet to the chest and I was completely overcome with so many new emotions.

All I could think was I need to hug my dad and tell him I love him too. I also wanted to thank him for sacrificing for us and let him know that we accepted and appreciated his effort. So many emotions ran through my mind at that moment. Then I remembered, Oh my God, I gotta go up there and say my speech now. I'm not gonna make it!

I took the stage after my dad and started sharing stories about my mom and the lessons she had taught me. I was talking about all of her accomplishments and funny anecdotes from my childhood. As I expected, I was having such difficulties getting through it. I couldn't get my words out without breaking down in tears. Even my professional training as an actor, being taught how to compartmentalize and visualize, didn't help me one bit at that moment. My vocal cords kept swelling up, choking out my words, like a vice grip. The constriction in my throat denied my words from flowing out of my mouth. I was a complete mumbling wreck.

Out of nowhere, I lifted my head, salty, relentless tears hampering my vision, and saw my son, Baron, was standing beside me like a solider on watch. There was something indescribable about how much stability he gave me in that moment. His physical presence changed the energy of the situation. He stood there putting his hand on me, steadying me enough to see my way through to the finish line. His presence gave me peace and levity; it grounded me in reality. The roles reversed and he was fathering and nurturing me. I felt like I was spiraling downward, out of control at that moment, and Baron saved his pops for real! I would never have made it through that speech without him. In that moment I got a glimpse of the empathetic and caring man I had created, the one who would carry on my own legacy. It made me so damn proud!

Afterward, Baron confessed, "Daddy, I've never seen you like that before. I've never seen you cry, Daddy!" I could hear the fear and shock in his voice.

I said, "It's okay, it's all right. I'll be okay now. Thank you, son. I love you!"

The day seemed so surreal. I still remember when they lifted the cage doors and released a bunch of white doves into the bright blue sky. The contrast was miraculous and made all the day's events seem so final. Afterward, guests slowly walked back to their cars, sharing their condolences with me. I was numb. I was in a robotic mindset during the rest of the day when the family gathered at the repass ceremony. I was physically there, but mentally I was far, far away.

I'll never forget that night when I went to sleep. I didn't know if I was going to wake up the next day. With the excruciating hurt I felt, I honestly questioned if I had just lived my last day. Not knowing if I would be able to continue my life was the craziest feeling in the world to me because I was always an optimistic dude. Always able to rationalize and put everything to a plan or into perspective. Not this time. I had no plan and I had lost all perspective on life. I felt completely disassembled.

The only thing that saved me was the normality of life. I had to take my kids to school; I had to read scripts. I had to do all these different things that provided the distraction I needed to function under extreme pain. I put one foot in front of the other and took baby steps back to living and experiencing life again. Even now, some days I get a setback, then I have to remind myself it's only temporary and I'm still here for a purpose. And then, some days I smile and laugh because I'm so proud to have that experience, to have had the mother I had. Life is about perspective.

Most recently, in 2021, I lost my cousin Derrick Bellamy after spending one of the most fun-filled weekends together. We had a blast catching up and laughing together like we did when we were kids. Our time together was filled with pure carefree joy! Once again, his sudden death was a shocking reminder to stay present, love constantly, and fearlessly.

Life today has come full circle for me. My sister and I care for my dad who is struggling with old age and his own declining health issues. It never gets easier, and unfortunately, I've had the practice of having to navigate around those issues. Karen is my copilot and my rock when it comes to caring for my dad. He too has his stubborn ways, keeping us both on skates. The difference with him is that we can usually tag team and get him to see things our way. I wish my mother had been like that.

Over the past few years of the pandemic, everybody has had to face their own mortality and figure out how to live life more purposefully. I know I've had those talks with myself, and it has made me a better man. I don't sweat the small stuff anymore, and I damn sure don't let opportunities pass me by, thinking they'll swing back around again.

I am here today for a purpose and I resolve to use all my energy to figure out how to meet that purpose head-on with intention. I vowed to continue to show up as a dad and friend to my young adult kids. To continue to show up with an abundance of love and support to my beautiful wife, Kristen, knowing that we have each other and have built so much together even when times and schedules are challenging. To show up in a loving and nurturing way to my aging father and my beautiful sister, Karen. And to show up for me, Bill Bellamy, because I know I am worth it too.

That's what successfully mastering life looks like to me today! Life has taught me that love is essential to us all. Our pure existence cannot sustain itself without it. Loving ourselves and forgiving ourselves are incredible tools we need to sharpen for a successful existence in this life. I hope that it will be known forever that I was never afraid to love my people. We are everything.

God blessed me with this gift for generating laughter. I will continue to share it with the world as long as I may live!

16

MY FATHER'S SON

___

When I think of my father's life, three profound words come to mind: compassion, generosity, and kindness.

The passing of William Bellamy on June 24, 2022, just as I had wrapped up writing the final chapter of this memoir, rocked my world. It was only after he was gone that I realized how much it pained me that he would never get to read a word of what I wrote. I would never get to hear him say, one more time, how proud he was. That he would never get to completely understand my full-circle realization that I am my father's son.

My dad lived a relatively good life. He was able to accomplish so much with so little. A hard-working man with an incredible sense of family. That's what he was and what I have become. My dad was a simple country boy born on the dirt roads of Cottondale, Florida. A man with just a high school education who had overcome so much against all odds.

Whether it was for his immediate family, or his family of friends, Dad always extended a helping hand. Stopping by just to make a friend laugh. Picking up a friend when their car broke down, or fixing their car and joking with them that "He can't fix no car past '95 because they put the computer on it and you can't get up under there no more." He never complained in life; he just met whatever challenge head on and did his best. He would always tell me, "Bill, if you do it right the first time, you don't have to go back and do it again." No complicated words, just pure truth and profound honesty—that's what he represented. His youthful and curious outlook on life always made me laugh. He'd ask the most random questions that would disarm you in an instant. That's where I inherited my goofy curiosity from. He'd randomly ask, "Billy, you don't ever get scared flying in the air all the time? You ever think about the earthquakes in California? How you have all that energy to take care of your family and your career and keep a smile on your face?" Then he would sit back, run his hand across his low-cut hair, and say, "Boy, you a hell of a man. It's no easy task. You cut for it!" He showed love and cheered me on in his own way. One afternoon he called just to tell me he could not believe how big my billboard was in Times Square. "Boy, who would have ever told me I would ever see my boy in the middle of New York City? This is big time, Billy! Only the big people get up there." He was my one-man band. My built-in hype man, my original ride or die. I grew up with so many friends and acquaintances that either hated their pops or didn't know them at all. I was blessed to call mine my best friend.

The first time I ever heard my dad cry was actually weird and hilariously traumatic if you can picture how it all played out. I'd never gotten four back-to-back missed calls from my dad before so when I did, I knew something strange happened. Calling him back, I anxiously stated, "Daddy, what's wrong?"

"He gone, Bill, he gone. The dog's gone. He got hold of something, or somebody poisoned him. That dog ain't do nothing to nobody, you hear me? He was a good damn dog. I gotta do something with him!" My dad proceeded to tell me that he had been wandering around Newark desperately trying to find somewhere to lay his dog to rest.

"Daddy, you driving around town with a dead dog?" I asked him, dumbfounded by the picture of him carting it around in the back of his truck. He was such a nurturer and he cared so deeply—with all his heart and soul. Even for his raggedy old dog and I loved him for it.

I am a proud daddy's boy. My dad is and was my hero. I admired his big hands, gold tooth, and all his funny sayings. I can tell you every car my daddy drove and the sound the engines made. I always knew when he pulled up in front of the apartment. I would sit in the window waiting for him to come home from working his two jobs. He'd step out of his car, crane his neck to look up to our small apartment, and there I'd be in that window looking down, marveling at a warrior returning from a hard-fought battle!

As I sit here today, mourning that warrior's passing from my life, I honor him by celebrating and remembering all that was good about his life and the legacy he left us with. I reflect on how I can live my life, so my kids see me as their hero. I remind myself to be confident and comfortable in my own skin, regardless of what's going right or wrong. To own whoever I am and to continue to be the best I can be. And, most of all, to

keep life simple because it doesn't have to be any more complicated than that. My dad embodied these characteristics in his
life and always lived by example.

William never spoke a bad word of anyone, but he would
always tell you his honest take on a situation. The unique personality nuances of all his children were crystal clear to him.
With laser precision he knew exactly how to engage with each
of us differently and truly listen. He hardly vocalized words
of love early in his life, but he showed it through his steady
daily acts of caring. The tender patience he practiced nursing
my mom when her health became compromised left me in awe.
Most people couldn't have mustered the strength to walk that
torturous road. Yet, he did and those who knew my mom well
knew the job was no easy task. It was his commitment to his
vows that kept him faithful to his purpose, he confessed to me.

The running joke I had with my dad was that he had nine
lives, just like a damn alley cat. The man surely had a guardian
angel who worked overtime guiding his steps. Let me elaborate. He was set on fire; he survived. He was electrocuted; he
survived. A car fell on his chest while he was working under
it; he survived. My dad had a stroke; he survived. Found out
he had a clogged artery that needed a stent. During surgery
it opened up on its own, nearly killing him on the table; he
survived that surgery. He fell and broke his hip; he recovered!
This man was like Superman in my eyes. Nothing could defeat
him. That's why when he was rehabbing for his hip, I told him,
"You are getting out of this place because that's what you do.
You conquer!" He called me every day to share his progress
right up until he was finally released. I brought him to California to continue his healing. Not only did he walk again, I
witnessed his confidence soar because he thought he wouldn't

ever get back to "normal." Every morning we'd take our daily walk through my local park, talking about old times and commenting on the predictable dry heat that Californians love to hate. One day on our walk, he shocked the heck out of me by putting down the walker and leaving me in the park, mouth hanging wide open, marveling at his newfound independence and strength.

The last few years had not been kind to my dad, health wise. He was diagnosed with lymphoma and fighting like a champ to treat it aggressively. Numerous falls and tumbles were met with countless angels like Kyle Little, who just happened to visit and check in on my dad, rescuing him from being immobile on the floor for hours. Angels like my cousin Stephanie Bellamy, who called my dad on that day and recognized something wasn't right with him. My angelic uncle, Nathan Bellamy, who stayed by dad's side during his battle with COVID-19. In the process Nathan contracted COVID-19 himself and nursed my dad, and himself, back to health—Supermen! Now, that's true brotherhood!

Even though he knew he would not win this latest battle, my dad (my hero) still never gave up. Weeks before his death, when I visited with him, he told me to personally thank some specific people when his journey was done. Uncle Nathan Bellamy, Carl Bellamy, John Carlo, Diane Bellamy, Aunt Martha Anderson, and my devoted sister, Karen Bellamy.

My dad left this earth with a hopeful perspective. In our last talk he reminded me that bitterness was the enemy of happiness. That everyone should forgive and let bygones be bygones because life was too short for foolishness. I will carry his wisdom with me forever.

Dad's passing was thankfully not a tragic one. No murder or horrible car accident to leave me aching far more than I already am today. It was a quick and peaceful passing on his own terms. Cancer robbed him of his vitality, but did not consume his sharp wit or curious mind. Until his last breath, William Bellamy gave us laughter and memories and was still full of pride.

In my opinion, he still beat cancer! In true Bellamy form, he still won! He touched us all in his own unique way. And that, my friends, is the true Bellamy legacy. Thank you, Daddy, for teaching me to be a worthy man.

ACKNOWLEDGMENTS

For those who I may have left out, just know it's a lapse in memory and not a lapse of intention.

My family has always provided the structure on which I've built my foundation. One roof, many walls, and a bunch of angles. Today this structure has been tested and even torn apart, yet our foundation is still strong!

My brother, Julius, taught me the hard reality that life is too short and health too fleeting. Seize the day, nurture your body, and live fearlessly. I love you baby bro, and I will continue to honor your playful and curious spirit throughout my own life. I miss you.

Mommy and Daddy, life without you as my anchors will be difficult, but unavoidable. You prepared me for the realities of what this life can bring and it sustains me in your absence.

Karen, you are my only sister and have been everyone's caretaker. Now it's your time to explore life selfishly, fueled with a renewed self-purpose. I will always be here to support you in any way you need.

Eternal love and awe for my soul mate and wife, Kristen Bellamy. You have been my spiritual backbone and safe harbor for over twenty amazing years! Unwavering in your support of my dreams, and unshakable in your faith, you've masterfully created a beautiful life for our family. You made me a father, and I am humbled by your constant sacrifice. I appreciate you in every way. Bailey Ivory-Rose and Baron, thank you for all that you have taught me. My journey as a dad made my life worth living in ways I never knew existed. My love for you knows no boundaries.

Huge shout-outs overflowing with respect and honor to my uncles Nathan Bellamy, Randolph Bellamy, Carl Bellamy, James Roy Bellamy, Allen Blaine, Ivory Hall Jr., and John Robertson. To my aunties Elizabeth, Diane Bellamy, Eugina, Eloise, Elise, and Martha Anderson; it takes a village of support and I thank you all for pouring wisdom into me while nurturing and guiding my steps throughout different phases of my life.

Ron Workman, you have been a true brother from day one! As my friend and my first road manager, you've always served up pure raw honesty, friendship, clarity, and loyalty. Emory Ward, thank you for always having my back and showing me unwavering levels of friendship and loyalty. Terrance Thomas, your business-minded focus and experience have continued to keep our team on track and we love you for it, man.

Reaching way back to recognize my brothers from the schoolhouse crew: Martin Moore, Jacques Lucien, Brian Jackson, Dave McPherson, Frank Dookie, and Dewayne Dixon. We made it through the treehouse and created so many game-changing moments. We made it out of the house of dreams. Thanks for the memories and continued brotherhood.

Professionally, the first angel I need to thank is Tracey Jordan at MTV, who put me on the map and allowed me to showcase my talent on the world stage. Also, a huge thank you to Russell Simmons for his visionary genius and for seeing something in me at the iconic Uptown Comedy Club in New York City. Bob Sumner, my first manager, you believed in me so fiercely and consistently and saw potential and levels in my career I didn't see myself. You helped me nurture my talent so I could grow to become the comedian and entertainer I am today. You will always have a grateful copilot in me.

Mad respect to the Breakfast Club morning show: DJ Envy, Angela Yee, Charlamagne tha God. You may not realize it, but our crazy in-depth interviews spurred me to reflect on my contribution to the culture and breathed life into the idea for this memoir. Sometimes you can be too close to your own successes to fully realize their lasting impact. That's the truth—I thank you for helping me to embrace it!

To my fellow trailblazer, Kevin Powell—I thank you for being one of my brilliant peers. Like an assassin, you carved your own path while I was surgically orchestrating my own. As a brilliant writer, producer, and thought leader you are inspiring young Black men for generations to come.

To all the radio and TV personalities that have shown me support throughout my career; the love is real!

To Barry Katz, you've been one of my mentors and collaborators and an undeniable bright spot in my career.

Nicole E. Smith, my coauthor, thank you for sharing this journey with me. Organizing my thoughts and capturing my voice perfectly, you provided a safe space for me to tell my truths. This is our success!

Finally, to my comedy agents Tamra Goins, Jenny Kim, Matt Bourne, and Christina Shams—thank you for helping me to keep the world laughing.

ABOUT THE AUTHOR

Using his experiences growing up in Newark, Bill Bellamy started doing stand-up while he was a student at Rutgers University. Bellamy quickly discovered how much he enjoyed making people laugh and began honing his skills at small comedy clubs around the country and was soon making waves in the New York clubs such as The Improv, The Comic Strip, and The Comedy Store in Los Angeles.

Less than two years after launching his stand-up career, Bellamy earned a spot on HBO's *Def Comedy Jam*, where he notoriously coined the phrase "Booty Call." The now-famous late-night rendezvous moniker became the name of his first comedy special for Showtime. It was instantly one of the network's top-rated specials.

Bellamy became a staple on MTV in the '90s as one of the first "VJs" on the network. He hosted several of their programming blocks, including *MTV Jams*, *MTV Top 20 Countdown*, and *MTV Beach House*, while interviewing everyone from Kurt Cobain, Prince, and Snoop Dogg to Janet Jackson. In 1996, Bellamy landed his own late night series, *The Bill Bellamy Show*.

Bellamy starred in and executive produced his own syndi-
cated show in 2012 called *Mr. Box Office*, with costars Jon
Lovitz, Tim Meadows, and Vivica A. Fox. Prior to *Mr. Box
Office*, Bellamy appeared on recurring episodes of Tyler Perry's
Meet the Browns (on TBS) and has guest-starred on ABC's *Castle*,
USA's *Royal Pains*, USA's *White Collar*, and TNT's *Murder in the
First*. Previously, Bellamy hosted and produced four seasons of
the TV One comedy competition show *Bill Bellamy's Who's Got
Jokes?* and hosted two seasons of NBC's Emmy-nominated *Last
Comic Standing*.

Bellamy also continued to star on the big screen in addition
to garnering coveted guest roles in several prominent televi-
sion series. Bellamy starred in *Love Jones, Def Jam's How to
Be A Player, Love Stinks, The Brothers*, and *Any Given Sunday*.
Bellamy continued to hone his comedy and stand-up prowess.
He debuted his second comedy special, *Crazy Sexy Dirty*, in
May 2012. It was one of the highest rated comedy specials on
Showtime in the following years. In 2017, Bellamy costarred
with Shemar Moore and Nadine Velazquez in the romantic
comedy *The Bounce Back*.

Bellamy was a recurring cohost on *The Rachael Ray Show*
and has also filled in for host Mario Lopez on *Access Hollywood
Live* and hosted the ESPY Awards red carpet for *Entertainment
Tonight*.

Bellamy decided return to his first love—stand-up comedy.
He debuted his third Showtime comedy special, *Ladies Night
Out*. The tour sold out nationwide and featured material by
comedians Ali Siddiq, Jay Reid, and D'Lai. In 2017, Bellamy
also headlined a nationwide comedy tour, the Standing Ovation
Tour, with Tommy Davidson, Sommore, Marc Curry, and Tony
Rock.

Bellamy joined the top-rated *Tom Joyner Morning Show* as a weekly cohost for the 2017 season.

In 2018, Bellamy had a key recurring role on HBO's *Insecure*. Bellamy also starred in the horror/thriller film *A Dark Foe* opposite Selma Blair and Graham Greene. He also landed a series regular role in the ABC pilot *Nana* alongside Katey Sagal. Bellamy produced and starred in the holiday film *A Rich Christmas* for BET+ while starring in the comedy *Back on the Strip* featuring Wesley Snipes, Tiffany Haddish, J. B. Smoove, Gary Owen, and Faizon Love. He also signed a joint venture with Breakbeat Media to produce his own podcast called *Top Billin'*.